BUDGET CONSIDERATIONS

Budget Considerations

Lawrance George Lux

Writers Club Press

San Jose New York Lincoln Shanghai

Budget Considerations

Writers Club Press
an imprint of iUniverse, Inc.

For information address:
iUniverse, Inc.
5220 S. 16th St., Suite 200
Lincoln, NE 68512
www.iuniverse.com

ISBN: 0-595-22096-7

Printed in the United States of America

Contents

Preface

The Author begins this Work with great doubts; the Issues involved are so huge, they functionally defy one Individual's effort. The United States Federal Government stands as the largest Employer in the World, unmatched even by Russia, China, or India. This does not include State and Local American governments, which effectively double the number of Government employees in this Country. Others would contest the above statements; yet We remain the most inefficient Country in the World, with more Civil Servants per Million Citizens than any other entity.

The Federal Judiciary employs more personnel than the entire government functionaries of most Countries, with Populations of less than Thirty Million. The State Judiciaries, when including the practice of Public Defendants, employ almost Eight times the personnel. Public funding of Education spurs a huge increase in Government employment; more personnel are employed by American School Boards than the entirety of personnel employed in the British Judicial system. America hires more road maintenance personnel than military personnel employed by NATO, ranking only 11th in the quality of roadways. Total Government employment, whole or partial, undoubtedly exceeds Twenty Million; when considering Janitors, Librarians, Teachers, Social Workers, Military and Military Contractors, Law Enforcement officers of all types, and employed Convicts in the Penal system. This is the Windmill the modern Cervantes attempts to joust.

U.S. Government obviously maintains the position of largest Employer in the World. Salaries and Pensions exceed the GDPs of many nations of the World. They collectively allocate a Retirement

Fund which is larger than the total Government revenues of France; and examined in detail, are on average only 14th in the quality of Pension funds in the area of providing personal security. Pension fund employees, when including the Social Security administration, draw salaries and benefits in excess of the Government budgets of any African nation.

All Government employees, Federal, State, and Local, possess a standard of living, though, inferior to the Civil Servants of any NATO nation; when compared to the standard of living of the average Citizen in the employer nation. Financial charges for administration of Government salaries and Pensions in the United States, exceed the financial charges demanded by the entire Swiss banking system. Largess does not suggest success, and lack of central policy shown by the misallocations found in the administration of Government Service.

An aware Reader may have noticed We have not reached discussion of what most consider the primary issues of the Budget: the rampant use of Pork Barrel, the huge expenditure to the Military/Industrial complex Companies, feather-bedding in government bureaucracy, infrastructure contracting inefficiency, Cost Overruns, competing and conflicting programs, excessive Project funding, the inability to kill any Program no matter it's obsolete nature, duplication of effort between Agencies or levels of government, mirage employment, inefficiency of Civil Servant labor, COLAs, lack of quality control, payment for research and production even when product denied, military and Civil Service overstocking of supply, and the theft of Government property and funds.

The Author's friends wanted him to write this Book; he obviously does not need enemies.

1

Overview

The President of the United States supervises the largest Organization in the World, if the term supervision is used very loosely. The Problem can be defined in another way: A Special Committee of the United States Congress was delegated some years back; their sole purpose was to study and close unneeded military bases and properties. The Committee enjoyed huge success, though most of their proposals failed to be ratified by Congress itself. The interesting datum issued by this Committee, was the little observed item where they suggested they had found 97% of the military properties in the United States. This was the actual land owned by the United States military.

The Defense Department suffers from a lack of current records, and many areas were closed before the First World War. The Secretary of Defense believes He knows the location of Eighty percent of the Warehouses of the Military. One ingenious Defense Accountant estimates Inventory still includes 200,000 tires produced for WWI, and Two million tires produced for WWII. It is believed there are 200 fully-equipped MASH medical units still existent in warehousing, circa 1945. This Work, though, is not a tirade against the U.S. Military.

It can be estimated there are at least Twenty Supply warehouses unvisited since the movement of Department headquarters to new locations, circa 1970 and previous. There exist Federal office buildings, where no living Soul has been within the premises since before 1950. The Author once talked to a Security Guard, who had been hired to check a Federal building after it was closed. He shares the detail with two other Guards, and has been on the job for 24 years. Both the Military and the Civil Service has tendency to move on, and forget about old problems and locations. The Central Intelligence Agency still owns two untenanted buildings in the D.C. area, which they abandoned with movement to Langley, Virginia. The State Department still owns a home in San Francisco, lasted used in 1905.

The Federal Government has not had a complete Inventory ordered, since the Grant administration; which was considered to be only Ninety percent accurate. The Defense Department cannot determine the exact expenditure pattern of some Two Trillion dollars. The State Department still cannot account for Aid program Fund expenditures, allocated in the 1960s; the Cash is gone. It can be asserted some Two years of Taxes paid since 1940, cannot be found by any accounting procedures. It is assured a lot of people made a lot of money.

Vice-President Al Gore, in his first term, made a serious effort to account for all employees of the Federal Government. He could come up with a Name, Face, and Work location for only about 98% of the total; though the Clinton administration made it a high priority. Al Gore found real resistance to the effort, emanating from the Agencies and Departments. Mirage employment remains quite high, as an estimated means for middle-level department heads to supplement their income.

They run hires on the Books, send the checks to specified locations, and cash the checks themselves. The most common practice occurs in failure to turn in Letters of Resignation, and simple transfer of mailing address for the salary checks. The IRS does not catch the Ruse, if the department head does not forward the proper salary list. The only danger remains if the former employee notices an enhanced Social Security payment. Most would say this practice could not be maintained, yet department heads who retired up to Twenty years previously, may be getting five or six retirement checks per month.

A second common ploy consists of designating family members as qualified for benefit packages, under a department social program. One instance discovered was of a department head awarding housing subsistence payments to five members of his own household. He purportedly rented to each of the five members of his family, at a rate of $370 per month. It was discovered because of the common address of rental. Most department heads are familiar with common research procedures for Fraud control, and do not act in such a stupid manner.

Another device is to artificially inflate Expenses, where such Expenses are to be expected. One department head at an OSHUA district listed approximately 8,000 miles of travel per month from all Employees at $.35 per mile. Actual travel by district employees gained by personal interrogation, indicated less than 200 miles of travel per month. Some of the employees had not been out of the office in years. The department head billed national headquarters for the total amount, then issued individual checks. The fraud was discovered through the common endorsement on most of the issued checks; the department head's wife endorsing all the checks. Examination of the checks indicated the fraud was over many years duration.

Many other opportunities exist for fraud. A major department head in a Midwestern City made a deal with a Manager of a Office Supply company. The Company found the fraud. The Manager was listing the supplies as sold Wholesale, while billing the department full retail price. The department head would write the check, which the Manager deposited the check into a account with the Office Supply Company name; but accessible only by the Manager. The Manager would then write a check to the proper account of the Office Supply company, and a check to the department head for half the difference in Price. The false Account name served to pacify both the Office Supply Company and the Treasury. The gain was an estimated $2000 per month, for the department head and Manager. The false Account had been open for Sixteen years.

Aid Managers and Military department heads are often accustomed to Kickbacks in the issuance of Awards. It is common knowledge retired Military officers often go to work for Military/Industrial complex companies, when they had been supervisory bursars of military funds to these Companies in their military service. What is unknown about this after-retirement employment, comes in the pre-set length of this after-retirement employment; determined prior to retirement from military service. Ninety-five percent of all Aid Fund Dispensers have historically held personal accounts in foreign bank accounts, three times the average of normal Foreign Service personnel, outside of temporary accounts held while in a specific country. Eighty-five percent of military officers who take senior Management positions with Corporations; do so with Companies who they supervised in Weapons technology development, or Procurement activities.

Chicanery remains rife in Government service, but it is only the tip of the Iceberg. These activities do not account for the 'lost funds'; most of these activities are listed as expenses, in one manner or another. The most important source for loss of funds come through departmental discretionary expense accounts. One of the most simple extortions ever listed, was conducted by a simple Corporal assigned to vehicle service at the Pentagon. Generals often sent him to wash their military-assigned car. The Corporal simply told the aides to the Generals he needed money to wash the vehicle, and often withdrew the money from the aide's drawer himself. He always took a hundred dollar bill, then drove a local vehicle maintenance military shop, where enlisted personnel did the job for nothing. He repeated the procedure, when the vehicles needed to be fueled, signing normal military fuel dispersal sheets to get the gas for nothing. Aides to Generals are normally issued discretionary expense accounts, and habitually spend between $30,000-80,000 apiece from these accounts per year. Most of the funds from these accounts are spent in a like manner as to that described above.

The trappings of Power also cost an excessive amount. Senior Military officers and high rank Civil Servants often retrieve family members for Holidays; the only requirement being a local military airport. The cost of Civilian air transport remains quite excessive, when compared to military air transport paid by military budget. A crude estimate would suggest over Twenty thousand Government functionaries involved in this practice.

Even middle-rank military officers and all senior Civil Servants stay in the costlier Hotel suites when in Washington; places which they would abandon to a Holiday Inn, if paid for by themselves. It was once estimated by this errant Author, the average cost of a meal for an Out-of-Town Government functionary cost the American taxpayer around $30; he has eaten a Burger King hamburger for $1.25 within sight of the Capital building. These functionaries join the Author at Burger King, when at home.

The Reader probably begins to think this Monologue provides a boring exercise, which does not endorse the real root of Budget duress. The Reader could not be further in error. Such practices as described above, account for not less than Six percent, not more than Eleven percent, or the total yearly expenditure of Federal Budget per year. The size of the Federal Budget is climbing toward Two Trillion dollars per year. The Reader needs to pull out his Calculator, and start punching numbers; be careful with the proper placement of zeros!

It is indicative of the problem to state middle-rank and Senior Government functionaries travel about Twelve times the total miles of their Counterparts in foreign Governments; the usual number of nights spent in hotel or motel accommodations stands at 14-57 nights per year, depending on rank. The average number of air miles is clocked at around 57,000 per year. The number of Personnel engaged in this activity approaches 300,000. All of the above expenses are borne by the American taxpayers. The Secret Service Expense accounts alone, exceed the Government budgets of some States. These Government paid Vacations serve as one of the Perks of Government service.

Another annoyance for American Taxpayers must be Civil Service regulations. Paid Vacation leave paid for Government employees exceeds the gross revenues of General Motors. Paid Sick-days for Government employees easily exceeds the daily Employee wages of the self-same General Motors. Certain Studies, quite unofficial, estimate Civil Servants spend less than Six hours per workday at their desk or Post, compared to 7+ by their private counterparts. A creditable Study compared Output based upon the paperwork crossing the desk of employees. Private employees processed approximately Seven reports per hour; Civil Servants averaged that number per day.

Private employees can be fired within a day; Civil Servants require a lengthier process, the minimum time for Federal employee of over Three years service is Seven months, with up to a 36 month Review process. There are certain Federal employees, based on their seniority, who can receive Three months of Vacation, plus Three months of Sick leave, Six weeks of Compassionate leave, and 60 days of outside-study training leave without losing a dime of Pay, and possessing the highest pay scales of the Civil Service. Civil Servants traditionally take approximately twice the Vacation time, and Three times the Sick leave, as their Private counterparts.

The Military/Industrial complex Companies present a debacle to American Taxpayers. A famous News Network has been using the term 'Reality Check'. The area of Military Weapons procurement needs such a check. There is incredible fanfare about new 'Smart Weapons'. This concept exceeds the terminology. 'Smart Weapons' are first of all not new. They have been around since the late 1970s, in some form. The age of these weapons have relevance to the discussion of Expenditures.

'Smart Weapons' are actually not smart; they are actually very dumb, doing absolutely nothing more than what they have been programmed to do. These weapons remain only Computer-assisted targeting weaponry. Target assessment by Computer faces constraints by the inadequacy of program development, and the lack of Sensor capacity.

These constraints save many Pilots' lives; Pilots who study religiously the fallible nature of Computer-assisted targeting. They learn to utilize the common failures of Computer-assisted targeting, or die. The success of Air War against Our enemies during the last Two conflicts, indicates they have learned the lesson well.

The Patriot Missile System Defense is probably the most advanced Computer-assisted targeting system currently in use. Pentagon Spokespersons proclaim an Eighty percent interception rate for the Patriots. Trade people estimate the interception rate is closer to Fifty percent. A discussion of Who is right stands as futile; Everyone can agree there remains a 20-30% loss of Target acquisition and destruction. The Author wishes to state this figure is an excellent record for a military weapon system; prime statistics for military use and dispersal. How does this relate to military expenditures?

Nine weapon systems now under examination and development, to supercede or complement the Patriot system, all utilize Computer-assisted Targeting acquisition. The Author enjoys most One which is a Pickup-transported anti-aircraft system with munitions trailer, which he believes will greatly enhance the power of the standard military division. The Rockets are small for easy transportation, and repeat firing sequence so rapid as to be acceptable with a 92% destruction rate. The system suffers from certain defects, both machine and human error.

The Rockets do not discern between Enemy and Friendly aircraft, unless Friendly aircraft carry continuous pulsar beacons; interruption of said signal bringing friendly craft down. The second is a required mechanical arming system, so as not to set off the rockets on the munitions trailer. The Human error enters in attempts to provide a ground role to the system. Friendly transport need the prerequisite beacon, which must function; and Computer-assisted targeting against ground targets remains as effective as line-of-sight targeting of 105mm howitzers. This amplifies one of the problems of weapons procurement: the tendency to overreach because of the huge expense of development.

All of the Nine weapons systems mentioned above, suffer from poor performance records in initial testing. Military and Research personnel proclaim such is always common to new weapons systems. This is admittedly true! The problem resides in the fact they allow the subject to drop, after the reward of future funding for redesign. What is the exact Parameters of the redesign?

Study of these systems indicate the performance of these systems improve, as the programming for the weapons systems begins to resemble the programming of the Patriot Missile system. The Patriot system stands as a success, because it is developed program which maximizes the capability of the Hardware, and minimizes the incapacities of the target acquisition by Sensor and programming. Sensor resolution capacity has hit a performance ceiling, and machines cannot think.

All Nine systems must effectively become a duplication of the Patriot system, to enjoy a performance success equal to the Patriot system. There can be little expected cure of the deficiencies of the Patriot system by the newer weapons systems, and all programming for all of the systems is for air defense, and little use for ground defense. The development of Cruise missile technology and 'Smart bombs' suffer from exactly the same limitations.

The above discussion indicates the general weapons procurement failure of the U.S. Military. Intense effort is directed towards new weapons research, even though old systems possess proven reliability. New weapons systems fail to meet performance standards, until they redesign to imitate the older systems; they are reputed to replace. The rationale for the concentration on weapons systems development derives from the power of the Military/Industrial complex Companies.

Older weapons systems are subject to production economies of scale. Production of these weapons can be effected at decreasing cost, with replacement parts for such systems reducing drastically in cost. Military/Industrial complex companies find a shrinking Profits picture off reduced total volume, through production of proven, older weapons systems. Research and development of new weapons systems stand as an open-end cash fund; amazingly increased with Cost overruns—which currently average approximately 375% over initial projections first approved by Congress. Military/Industrial complex Companies like new weapons system, and hate production of older weapons systems; their Campaign contributions to Congress and Presidential Candidates reflect this fact.

The Author will make a short aside to examine the military posture of the United States. B-52s are still the best heavy bombers We have; We need the production of 450 more new ones. The F-14 remains the best air defense Fighter We have, because they can be produced cheaply in great numbers; all National Guard squadrons should be equipped with these craft. We will need Swarm Fighters, if We ever confront a Power with an effective Air Force. The A-10s are still the best ground support bombers to have ever been in the U.S. arsenal; We need 2000 new ones.

The M-1 Abrams Tank is too large, too unmanuverable, and requires excessive Shop maintenance. We need 4000 new battle tanks, of the Thirty-ton range. The M-16 rifles in common deployment must be replaced with a modified version of the M-14 rifle. The M-16 was designed for Jungle warfare, and works poorly elsewhere. The greatest detriment is the lack of bullet mass, and inability to provide accurate cone-fire over distance, for suppression of enemy movement and action.

The reliance on Helicopters for transport is foolhardy, when confronted by a technologically efficient Enemy; We need 4000 armored Personnel carriers, and 8000 straight military transport trucks. The Author finishes with the demand for 2000 more self-propelled 105mm and 155mm howitzers; self-propelled artillery did far more to win WWII, than did the Sherman tank; or even the T-34 Russian tank.

A return to the real subject of the Work in progress, must investigate the use of Pork Barrel. Operation of the American political system not only produces a huge amount of excessive spending on local projects to raise local area incomes and profits; it also generates the worst effects of such spending. Outright Pork Barrel, expenditure with actual little long-term value to the area or national economy, probably constitutes almost Ten percent of the current budgets. George W. Bush desires the first Federal Budget in excess of Two Trillion dollars. The Pork Barrel in it probably will exceed 300 Billion dollars. The current demand for Home Defense allows a great slush fund for Pork Barrel. Economists will be interested in how much of the spending will be superfluous, only beneficial to Corporate Profits.

The major indictment of Pork Barrel for any Economist lies in the Condemnation of Private property for use by the Government. Federal, State, and Local Governments continue to build, taking valuable Commercial property out of Private hands, with little chance of the property ever returning to commercial use. Governments never sell what they have acquired. They are also known to produce the poorest utility of property, of any entities in the Nation. They combine this poor utilization with the highest expenditure on Property maintenance of Anyone. Government Pork Barrel means a high initial expenditure, with continued excessive upkeep costs. Maintenance Costs of Government property consistently equate to approximately Twenty percent of the total salaries of the Individuals working on site per year; in comparison to around Eight percent for Private business. Government properties have a record of Renovation above normal Maintenance Costs every 3.7 years; compared to 11 years for Private industry. The American Taxpayer pays for Pork Barrel long past the initial funding.

Government construction often does not plan for Growth or Expansion, generally deliberately. This allows for additional construction. Expansionary construction of Government facilities occurs at likely double the rate of Private enterprise, with no attempt to compact individual Work areas. The Condemnation of Private property reduces the Property tax base, applying pressure on all other Property-holders; which mostly results in the greatest pressure being placed on the Residential owners.

Infrastructure Pork Barrel can be the worst form of the disease. Such Pork Barrel rarely relieves Population or Traffic pressure in the area involved. This occurs because Construction companies find much higher Profit in new construction, as compared to Renovation or resurfacing construction. Congestion areas are left without adequate access, while outlying areas gain access to the already congested areas. Politicians accede to the Construction companies desires, because of their own desire to be known for new development, which draws more Votes. The actual long-term reduction of Employment in the areas deters no one.

Federal Government expenditures currently expand at approximately Eight percent per year. Politicians, especially Republicans, would have Voters believe this increase occurs mainly from the increased benefits given to Citizens. Such increased benefits to Citizens account for no more than Twenty percent of the increased expenditures. The rest, approximately Six percent of the total Budget, derive from the Cost Overruns built into Federal funding. The average Individual citizen probably gains some $20 per year, due to increased Federal spending. The average Company engaged in Cost Overruns probably gains $4 Million and up; depending on the exact type of Contract. The average Military/Industrial complex company probably gains $2 Billion per year from Cost Overruns. There was the famous example of a Federal Courthouse, originally funded for $4 Million; it came in at $134 Million after Eleven years.

It is not as if Politicians do not recognize what is going on; they could not fail to notice. The greatest Military Procurement boondoggle was a weapons system whose research was refunded Twenty-nine times for 700 percent on the initial Project definition, where only 1000 weapons were ever purchased—produced at 840% of the initial stipulated cost, because the Military found the weapon system of insufficient performance. The Weapon system was the Predecessor of the Cruise missile. The Cruise missile, itself, had Research costs almost 1200 percent of initial funding, and is produced for Seventeen times the initial projected Price. Stealth technology Research costs over the years, could have paid every elected Public officials' salaries in the entirety of this Country for Sixteen years. Cost Overruns are no small item in the Federal Budget, and Corporations recognize this fact through their Political Contributions every year. Only American Tax-payers could ignore such sums.

Congress tried some years ago passage of a Sunset law, to get rid of obsolete Government programs and offices. The most noteworthy element of the effort became it's absolute failure. There are still Federal offices which answer fewer than a hundred Citizen inquires per year. Some fully staffed offices, like Assay and Mineral Claims offices in Western States, simply have answering machines which Someone checks once a Week. Civil Servants still exist who have been drawing salary for Years, though they had not been assigned a Work area, when offices were moved many Years before. The Author personally knows of Radar Installations, circa WWII, which were supervised by a senior NCO for Forty years, though they were not used; retirement of the last assigned Army Sargent, led to abandonment as a new Supervisor was not assigned.

There are Federal Depositories for Government publications, which are open by appointment only; though there is a permanently assigned, paid Librarian. There are smaller, older Federal Courthouses without a appointed Federal Judge; yet they are still fully staffed with bailiffs and legal clerks. There is still a Small Poultry Farm Bureau, though modern Agricultural Dept. regulations have made such Farm product unacceptable for Commercial sale; the office get maybe ten calls per year, all wrong numbers. A Bureau of Statistics office exists, where enquiries are made concerning old records not transcribed to Computer; Nine Civil Servants have handled Fourteen inquiries in Fifteen years, Twelve of those inquires ended in failure to find the information sought. The List could go on and on, though it would be as senseless as the continuance of the Federal Employment in these areas; one estimate backed by no serious data, believes such type Federal employee rolls extend past 30,000 Employees.

Other Authors make much of the ridiculous Research grants extended by Federal Departments; decrying the huge expenditures for idiot information. One that interested was a Two Million Study to ask if People liked working for a living; it was found not to have high appeal. A Academic grant for $500,000, funded under the Clinton administration, asked if People thought other People were Crazier than they used to be. A Labor Department study currently still funded, asks Civil Service personnel (Federal) if they derive job satisfaction from their work; the answers come at about a day's pay per answer. Another still funded by the same Department, asks these same Civil Servants if they think their Work areas should have more recreational and exercise facilities. What do you think their answers are?

The Federal Reserve System currently has a Two Million dollar Study to determine Employee preferences as to work location; most Employees desire employment in the Southwest, with the Northwest and South about tied for Second place (Seventy percent of the Work is concentrated in the Midwest and Northeast). A Defense Department Study for Five Million dollars determined Military personnel would like three times the Leave, while another Study concerning Civilian employees found a desire for double the paid Vacation. The idiotic nature of Federal Research studies need not be explored further.

The entire subject of COLAs must be broached. A confident statement can be asserted, stating COLAs have never attained more than one Quarter of the Budget increase per year; since the first introduction of COLAs in the mid-1960s. Middle-level and Upper-level Civil Service salaries increased an average Seven percent per year, throughout the same period. Cabinet-level, Judicial, and Congressional aide salaries increased by almost Eleven percent per year, over the same period. Congressional and Presidential salaries resolve to almost a Fourteen percent increase per year in splurge advances over the same period. It is interesting to note the salaries of Journalists covering Washington

D.C. and Political issues increased at about the same rate as Cabinet officers. This was almost double the rate of other Journalists in the Country. Examination of the functioning of COLAs indicates their yearly increase actually fell about a percentage point behind the actual Inflation rate, through these years; the shortfall coming from a apparent manipulation of data upon the part of Civil Service Economists.

The theft of Government property remains a scandal, even to the Beltway; the term for Our national Capital, used by Insiders. New media occasionally run stories about the theft of military property and weaponry, more to thrill Citizenry than point out a major problem. The theft of military weaponry constitutes less than a half a percent of all Federal property stolen. The most interesting item missing stands as the military vehicles known as Humvees. New Ones sold on the Consumer market carry a Price tag of $75,000. Defense Dept. records indicate there are 80,000 missing Humvees. This would seem an incredibly high number, except the Humvee is the common utility vehicle of the U.S. Military, with an estimated 800,000 vehicles purchased. The numbers tell of one out of ten vehicles misappropriated. Military Police spend probably less than Ten percent of their time, in search for missing military transport. The question is raised: Where are these vehicles, Public Vehicle Departments of the combined States do not list this number of Humvees registered? There is obviously a Vehicle Theft Ring operating out of American military bases, with transport of vehicles Overseas.

Federal law enforcement agencies have closed down Seven Office Supply companies in the last Thirty years; their crime being selling stolen Federal Office supplies to Private business. Some outlandish estimates state almost Twenty percent of such supplies are stolen and resold. It remains embarrassing easy to order 5000 reams of Paper, when 2000 are needed; even easier to not even deliver the amount ordered, simply resell it. The purchase of printed forms by Federal agencies indicate Civil Service bureaucrats are particularly sloppy in filling out these forms; only about Two-thirds of the printed forms are ever filed. Some could estimate the forms were never printed in the first place; such practice could pay the printing costs of private printing for printing companies.

The failure rate of the most common type of Secretarial typewriter used by Federal employees seem to fail at a much faster rate than those of private enterprise; either the maintenance practice of Civil Servants is poor, or these typewriters are not replaced as often as stipulated. Civil Servants also seem to use Light Bulbs at a Thirty percent higher rate than Private enterprise, upon examination of order records. Office chairs also see a high turnover rate. Filing cabinets seem to be discarded every Two years. Every Civil Servant must also have Three desk mats underneath those office chairs. Computers are not so great a failure; Government uses antiquated Hardware and programs. The Process is helped, by the common practice of Civil Servants not to supervise storage; but to simply wait at their desks to sign the Receipt forms of delivery personnel.

The whole process of Federal acquisition of Service vehicles brings enlightenment. The Federal Government purchases Contract vehicles today, and does much of Private American business. They return the Vehicles at the same rate, with generally Thirty percent less milage on the vehicles than those of Private business, and generally in Twenty percent better shape. Federal agencies generally report a Thirty percent higher turnover cost, than is Private business average turnover rate. It remains unknown the exact number of Contract vehicles in use by the Federal Government, but can be estimated as over a Million per year.

The Federal Government has also taken to purchasing 'Complete Package' Contract vehicles, as Auto dealers inform these equipped vehicles are the only salable product; charges would be much higher in turnover, unless the vehicles were fully-equipped. This practice only adds about $2000 to the turnover cost. The Auto dealers are quite justified in this demand; they could resell the Contract vehicles for only about $4000 less, without the 'Complete Package' of Power Steering, Power Windows, Power Door Locks, Air Conditioning, Tinted Windows, and Powered Side Mirrors. Private Business also buys the 'Complete Package' vehicles; they simply do not pay the added $2000.

Maintenance personnel of Federal facilities endure a qualification hiring procedure, which ensures they are capable of handling all the requirements of Maintenance in the Facility. Their pay scales reflect this specialization. Their on-the-job performance differs from the Hiring practice. Federal facilities subcontract Sixty percent of Maintenance by Management order. Heating, Air Conditioning, Plumbing, Window Replacement, and Electrical Wiring are all subcontracted. Maintenance personnel are reduced to Quality supervision, often interrupted by Management scheduling of Tasks. Federal Maintenance becomes 'Feather-bedded'. The Cost of Federal Maintenance programs rises by Forty percent per year.

Federal excesses can be examined in alternate manner. Economists estimate Federal facilities have between 70-4000% excess Warehouse and storage capacity; depending on how much Military bases and Reserves are entered into the Estimate. Economists estimate the Federal Government has Thirty percent excess of office space, especially introducing standard Work space areas of Private business—excess office space would then constitute 420% of space needed. They estimate there is a Forty percent Labor Oversupply, in comparison with Private business standards. Economists estimate Wage and Benefits of Civil Servants exceed Private Business standard by at least Forty percent. Federal Civil Servant Productivity stands as the lowest in the Nation, with the highest per-item rate of pay. People thinking to curtail the Federal Budget must start with the description of function, as outlined in this Chapter.

2

History of the Budget

Americans always exhibited great ambivalence toward Government expenditures. Two of the stated Causes of the American Revolution by the Propagandists of the Period were Taxation and failure to provide for Colony defense. Historical examination indicates Colonists enduring much less real tax than the English themselves; estimates vary as to the exact rate, but common thought suggests the Colonists real rate of Tax was only about Twelve percent of the real Tax burden on the English citizen. The Colonists were simply opposed to Taxation of any type; indications of this expressed by Tax riots against the Continental Congress in Virginia, New York, and South Carolina between the Declaration of Independence and the ratification of the Constitution.

The protest of lack of protection for the Colonies bears great insight into the Issue as well. The British Government bore the entirety of the burden of garrisoning troops in America, while enjoining the Colonists to provide housing for the Troops, raising and paying like levies of Colonial militia, and sharing a percentage of the Cost of the levies of imported Troops. The Colonies never paid more than one Quarter of the cost of imported Troops at any time, and most times paid nothing at all. Colonial militias never equaled the number of imported troops, and were most often left unpaid by Colonial legislatures. The British Government actually paid about half the Funds dispersed to Colonial militias. Americans throughout history imagined they should get something for nothing, and the Political process should be the process to attain the something.

A common argument in Republican circles today states the National Debt is actually low, in terms of the GDP. They advance this argument as justification of Tax cuts, and expenditures on programs directly benefitting Business interests. They claim the Dollar is too strong in International markets, and increased National Debt would weaken the Dollar. Democrats are likewise enthused with increasing the National Debt, simply have an alternate agenda. Both still outline the 'Something for Nothing through Government Expenditure' philosophy portrayed in all of American history.

Keynesian theory holds a limited validity in the American experience, the American economy almost always expanded with increased Government expenditure, stagnated in periods of reduced Government expenditure. This only expresses a limited impact, without a sufficiency of detail. Other tendencies offer far more enlightenment, along with a program of action which could be a Template for Budget discussions. This Chapter will mainly discuss these tendencies. The Reader should be aware many of the advanced ideas are hotly debated among Economists and the Greater Society. This Work provides only one side of the Argument.

The first Concept must be the Placement of real tax impact. This translates into Budget concern, based upon whether Taxes effectively pay for the Budget, or deficit spending is utilized. Historical Economic data indicates Economic growth attained under conditions without deficit Government spending, exhibit greater resiliency and less chance of Recessive conditions being engendered. The Six to Eight Periods of Economic activity where the above condition existed, all reverted into Recessive conditions after deficit Government spending programs were initiated. The impact was almost immediate; started by the shortage of Money supplies, but continued through an unpaid draft upon economic resources.

Study of the entire history of the United States provide many infer-ences about the American Economy. Extended periods of deficit spending actually indicate a stagnation of the standard of living among American citizens. There is an actual expressed decrease in the standard of living of Americans, whenever the real tax impact is shifted to lower income levels of Taxpayers. An increased real tax upon the Wealthy actually provides the fastest increases in the standard of living. The best scenario exhibited by the American Economy is one where Govern-ment expenditures are high, paid by Taxes without deficit spending, and the real tax impact is increasing against the upper income levels in American society.

Study of American Recessions highlights a amazing factor; increased Government expenditures do not necessarily spur the Economy. The Periods of the middle 1930s and the 1970s most signify this effect. Government spending in both Periods was high; both generated by deficit spending. A economic spur should exceed success within a Three-year periodicity; neither Period expressed such a economic spur. Both Periods disprove a simple implementation of Keynesian theory. The growth in Employment remained only that of actual Government expenditure employment, without secondary employment growth. Industrial orders only increased by arithmetic progression, not geomet-ric progression; so no real economic spur could be noted. Real Eco-nomic growth began in 1938, solely because of the restructuring of the military posture of the United States. It increased real employment, both in military placement order fulfillment, and increases in military complement. Lend-lease identicalized an increase in foreign trade, leading to replacement of military weaponry. An interesting venue of this activity lay in an increase in the real tax impact upon all citizens, but especially the wealthy.

The above statement leads to interesting formulations. Income Tax was extremely low in the later 1930s. A substantial amount had to be earned, before a realistic tax was imposed. The real tax impact was based upon Excise Taxes, and Income Taxes upon the Wealthy. Citizens has to be purchasing new Products, or earning a substantial income, in order to fund the existent taxes. There was a real increase in total Tax revenues, which indicated a real increase in the real tax impact upon the Wealthy, and the Purchasers of New Goods. This signified an actual Wealth transference to the Poorer incomes. The spur to the Economy was almost immediate, and the Economy started to boom by 1940; by 1942, the Economy had reached levels of pre-1929. Much debate exists about the exact largesse of the Four-year Period—1938-1942; but this Author believes almost 34% of all Wage-earners left the Lower Class for the Middle Class. This did not occur from simple Government spending, but actual economic transfer of Wealth from the Upper Class to the poorer Classes brought on an economic spur to the Economy; this spur generating sufficient Industrial growth in four years, to raise one-third of all Labor to the Middle Class.

Government deficit spending occurred throughout the 1970s, then actually increased in the 1980s. The actual Standard of Living stagnated throughout the entire Period. The real GDP actually stagnated throughout the Period as well. There exists no real indication this deficit spending provided any economic spur at all, except for arithmetic progression of productivity engendered by Welfare payments. Evidence exists the spur to the Economy which led to the boom in the 1980s, came solely from Corporate price reductions to inflate Sales of their Products. The lessened Profit per Unit directly translated into an increase in the income of Lower income Classes. This increased income led to increased economic activity on the part of the Poor, bringing substantial increases to economic activity.

The Boom of the 1980s came to an end with the S&L Bailout. Study of the S&L failures provide great insight to the failure of the Boom. Loans issued by the S&Ls, and by Banks of the same Period, were awarded upon high Profits projections. The Profits projection were founded upon unrealistic economic activity levels, but also upon an enlarged Profits per Unit picture. The Latter amplifies what was occurring in the greater Economy, which finally killed the Boom. Business was trying to enlarge their Profits per Unit of activity. They were effectively curtailing the income levels of the lower Income classes, by the rise in Product prices. Economic activity started to slow. The Recession was the direct result of Business policy, desirous of an enhanced Profits picture.

Keynesian policy can be seen to be intrinsically in error; simple Government expenditures, whether deficit or funded by Taxes, cannot spur Economic activity in and of itself. There must be a real transfer of Income to the Lower Income Classes, in order for a realistic Economic spur to be introduced. Economic history indicates this transfer is best handled by fully-funded expenditure, be it Government expenditure or Private action. Die-hard Republicans need be aware Trickle-down philosophy must be actual Trickle-down transference of Income to the poorer Classes. Wealthy Classes do not provide economic activity, only fund that economic activity. Economic Spurs come from transfer of Wealth from Capital Aggregation activity, to Consumer Consumption activity. Government Economic policy which does not understand this fundamental function, will be doomed to failure.

Supply-side Economists attribute great importance to the Capital-Aggregation function; an importance which is misplaced. A modern Economy combined with a modern banking system eliminates almost all need for Capital-Aggregation activity. The expansion of the Economy can be increasingly accomplished through the loan against total demand deposits held by Consumers in the Economy. The additional Capital needs can be supplied by the internal finance policies of the modern Corporate setup. Government loans and deficit spending cover any leftover Capital Aggregation needs. The Private investor turns into a dinosaur; relegated to playing with Paper instruments issued by Corporations and Governments, and funding Insurance securities. The position of the Private Investor becomes an increasing fiction, as the maturation of the Economy occurs. This fiction, though, can insert very adverse consequences into the functioning of a modern Economy.

The current Economic Recession is a case in point. There has been a reduction of Production over the past year (2001). The reduction almost equals the loss of Production which occurred in 1930. Does this not terrify the Reader? It should not! The vital difference comes in the fact the current Economy is about Twelve times the magnitude of the American economy of 1930. Actual Production figures are higher than in 1995—a Boom year. The Economy remains in a Inventory sale-mode, and is already showing signs of Recovery. The Reader will ask why the hullabaloo over the Recession?

There is a common adage today, which says Everyone is invested in the Stock Market in one way or another; screaming about 401k plans, Mutual Funds, Stock Portfolios. Investors roar about the horrid loss of Wealth. We must go back to the use of a Reality Check. Total investment in Stocks make up about 7.8% of the total Wealth of this Nation. Investors will retain at least Four percent of the total Wealth of this nation, not matter how far South, the Stock Markets will eventually go. Approximately 70% of the Investors involved will lose at most the Stock dividends for a year or two, due to the price they originally paid for the Stock in question. The loss of Wealth stated by Most, is nothing more than the loss of Paper Profits acquired from a Balloon market. The Author laughs at the Investors, a huge number, who claim the loss of Millions; when they initially invested Thirty thousand dollars a decade ago. He also has little sympathy for 401k holders, who claim they lost all but a half-Million dollars; about double what they ever put into the investment program. The fact stands no one can claim a loss, if they have maintained an Eight percent per year average increase in their holdings; less than Three percent of total Investors can claim losses greater.

Supply-side Economists err in their belief of the power of the Capital-Aggregation function. The current reaction to the current Recession, simply clarifies the fraud of claiming importance for Paper financial instruments. They do not possess the power, once held in 1929. This is because of the loss of power for the Capital-Aggregation function. A modern Economy funds itself, through it's modern banking system. The independence of Corporate Management from Stockholders portrays this loss of power. The Government finds an increasing need to supervise the activities of Corporate Management, as Board of Directors and Stockholders fail in tests of power. Government economic policies become vital in the vacuum.

Return to Budget consideration states real Economic spur must include real transfer of Wealth from Capital Aggregation to Consumer Consumption. This entails a transfer of Wealth from the Upper Classes, to the Lower Incomes. The real tax impact, therefore, becomes a vital issue to any discussion of Government economic policy. Tax Policy has historically been the most effective economic instrument for Government to affect the Economy as a whole. Tarriffs originally allowed development of native industry; then moved on to provide real censure to the Slave Trade and King Cotton. War Profits taxation brought real increases in the Standard of Living of Labor engaged in the War industries, though they did little to stop war profiteering. Social Security funding brought the great advances of Medicine, though Medical company and Doctor like to claim they are injured by treating Medicare patients; the venue where all derive over Forty percent of their Income. Total paid Capital Gains, little more than Twenty percent of the stipulated rates, provided more Revenue to Government; than all the proceeds of Taxation prior to 1940. Proceeds from the Corporate Income Taxes, real tax impact running at 18% of stipulated rate revenues, constitute in total sums; a greater amount than was invested in this Country, prior to 1920—both in real and adjusted rates for Inflation. Total Individual Income Tax revenues per year exceed the total GDP of this Country before 1900 in real terms; individual complaints should recognize these Taxes have raised the Standard of Living by an estimated 780%, since that time. Intensive study of real tax impacts is the most important arena of any Government economic policy.

Tax structures remain the most controversial area of Government political debate. The humor of the Debate resides in the lack of interest for most Taxpayers. They estimate correctly, the Taxes must be paid; and is unlikely to diminish significantly under any proposal. The array of Government services establishes the level of Taxation; and Employees, the backbone of the Tax system expect no windfalls. Their real concern remains ease of reportage and payment. Their major concern should be the limitation of the tax breaks for their Employers.

The percentage of overall taxes paid by Corporations has been falling since WWII. The percentage of overall Federal taxation Corporations paid in the 1950s, was about One-third of the Total Taxes. The percentage dropped slowly throughout the 1950s, increased it's drop through the 1960s and 1970s, and plunged downward after the Reagan administration. It has reached such a state Today, the current Bush stimulus package has provision to pay Corporations rebates; when they have not paid Taxes in years. The stimulus package is actually Corporate welfare. The Author should state Corporations have already received several Billions of dollars in Rebates, for Taxes which they never initially paid. This largesse occurs as Republicans rant at the spendthrift nature of Welfare for the Poor.

A study of the current Rebate measure brings interesting properties to the discussion. The average Recipient of Welfare assistance among the Poor gain about $6300 per year, not counting Medicaid or other Health services. The Rebates to the Corporations could be viewed in two ways: per Employee or per Stockholder. The Rebates split among Employees mean an average benefit in excess of $30,000 apiece. Split the Rebates among Stockholders brings a great variance, depending upon the setup of the Corporate structure; Publicized Corporations get a Stockholder benefit of only $3700 per Stockholder, under publicized Corporations gain Stockholders a $40,000 benefit apiece. Recognize there are more under publicized Corporations gaining Rebates, than highly publicized Corporations. It stands as a remarkable Stimulus package.

Rancor belittles Everyone, and further comment upon the current Federal Budget and Stimulus Packages will be abandoned. The Discussion revolves around the history of Federal spending. This history has many lessons to teach; real reason most refuse to revert to it. The most remarkable element derived from it, stands as 'Economic Performance actually improves with increased real Tax impact.' A supposition by the Author decides it's rationale comes from the actual Taxes paid, and spent as a Consumer in the Private Market. The majority of Taxpayers cannot effectively support an increased real Tax impact; such an increase would lead to a decline in their Consumption, disaster for Government and Business both. A real Tax impact increase thereby means forcing a Tax increase upon the wealthier elements of Society. Such an Increase upon the Wealthy possess a number of economic connotations.

An increase in the real Tax impact to the Wealthier elements of Society means their assumption of payment of a greater share of Government consumption of goods and services in the Private Sector. This can mean a reduced tax impact for Poorer classes, or simply a deferment of Public debt. It entails, in either case, a rise in the purchase of Private Sector goods and services by the Wealthier elements of Society; traditionally known for restriction of such purchase, in favor of Investment. This brings a higher purchase of Private Sector goods and services; higher because of defraying the assumption of debt in that Purchase. Future Labor assets will not have to be employed, in payment of Debt. This is reduced future commitment of Labor resources, and therefore, an increase in future Income for the Poorer classes. All Taxpayers are better off, even with the increased Tax impact.

The economic ramifications of this reduction of Debt works out as greater Labor asset devotion to the production of Goods and Services in the Private Sector. Inflationary pressure is decreased, and deflationary pressure applied; the greater commitment of Labor to production insures greater production at less cost. This applies even if the real Tax impact has increased on all Income levels. Reduction of Investment levels by the Wealthy classes do not restrict Capital Aggregation through the action of modern banking practice; based primarily on Demand Deposit account levels.

The increase in Production will lower Prices, as mentioned before; but also decrease the pressure on Government for the provision of Welfare. The Wealthier elements of Society face an increased real Tax impact, and will apply greater pressure to reduce the provision of Government goods and services; in hopes of reducing the real taxes paid. The end-result will be a lessened real Tax impact upon All, due to a reduction of Government expenditure. This results in an enhanced Consumption pattern among the less Wealthy classes.

The above analysis may seem like Economic Theory alone, but the history of Government expenditures provides evidence. Government expenditures were not high prior to the First World War, though a review of the American Civil War also present similar evidence. Government expenditures increased dramatically during the First World War. A vast Debt was accumulated because of this expenditure. A real difference occurred with this assumption of Debt. Restrictions were introduced to reduced War-Profiteering; these restrictions in effect, actually increased the real Tax impact upon all classes, especially the Wealthy. The working classes for the first time assumed a great percentage of the National Debt, through the sale of War bonds of small denominations. There occurred a vast increase in the Gross Domestic Product, with resultant increase in the Standard of Living even in the War atmosphere.

The Recession following the First World War was softened by the redemption of the War Bonds issued in the War. The real Tax impact on all Classes was maintained during this Redemption Process, which was effectively completed by 1925. The elimination of the National Debt occasioned real pressure by the Wealthier elements, for reduction of the real Tax impact upon themselves. This was accomplished by

1927. There was an immediate start to a reduction of Consumption levels among the Working classes and Poor, while Inflationary pressure with Price rises became apparent by the middle of 1927. Consumption declined in the intervening level to the degree, by the spring of 1929, Warehouses were overstocked.

The wealthier classes had resumed the practice of utilizing Investment, rather than increased Consumption. This consisted solely in Paper Instrument investment; as is normal practice for established Wealth households. The Stock Market continued to rise, though Plants were already involved in Capacity reduction because of lack of orders. Merchandise was not moving through Retail outlets, because of Working class reduction in Consumption. Three Quarters of poor performance and low Stock dividends, coupled with advance warnings of a disastrous predicted Four Quarter Business performance; brought on the Crash of 1929. Normal Business management had been investing heavily in the Stock Market with their Operating funds, because of the lack of opportunity exhibited for real Capital investment, on account of the poor Consumption records. The Crash of 1929 brought an immense shortage of Operating funds; leading to horrid Plant closings and Layoffs.

The huge losses to Investment Capital for the wealthier elements, with their demand for real Tax impact reduction, led the Government to restrict expenditures, as well as provide Tax relief for the wealthier classes. The Country enters the 1930s in terrible position; Business performance was not to increase, until Warehouse inventories were significantly reduced; the Working Classes did not have the Cash to Consume, and the Wealthier constrained their Consumption practice to rebuild lost reserves. Noted Economists believe it was the adoption of Keynesian practice of Government spending by both Hoover and Roosevelt, which brought about the Recovery. This Author disagrees, he asserts it was the gradual purchase of excess Inventories through the sheer aging of previously-purchased Product which brought the Recovery. It is his estimation the Recovery would have been far advanced, if the Government had simply paid Business to sell their excess Inventories at half-price.

The Government bungled through the 1930s, not initiating real programs to start Private enterprise. The Economy was not going to recover effectively, until private industry was back on it's feet. Continuous effort produced were attempts to save private wealth, and provide Employment insufficient to increase Consumption—just able to provide the Necessities. The Government fell into the right mix, by the need to increase and arm the Armed Services. Thousands were taken into the Military, providing Government supply of goods and services for them and their families. Business was awarded effective Production contracts; guaranteed to provide real Profits, with thousands of real Consumption-producing jobs in these Manufactures. Real Consumption began to pick up, and Business normalized; though re-introduction of a real Tax impact on the Wealthy classes would have to await World War II.

The War, itself, produced a vast expansion of the Standard of Living, though unrecognized until after it's end. The restriction on Purchases during the Conflict, enjoined a high Savings ratio among the Working classes; higher than ever before in history. Most family households held 300% of the financial reserves ever held previously in history. The Country entered the War with only One in Four households belonging to the Middle Class; by 1950, Seven out of Ten households belonged to the Middle Class. This reversal of fortune came directly from the enjoined Savings demanded by the War. The huge Consumer demand for Goods after 1945, plus the huge needs of Europe; easily absorbed the returning Veterans into the Labor force, bringing a vast increase of Middle-income wealth.

The Boom was continued throughout the 1950s, due to the vast dislocation by the War to most of the other industrialized nations. America ended the 1950s with an average Household wealth some Seven times as large as in 1940, even adjusted for the Inflation rate. The Individual Plant laborer was still saving approximately Three

Weeks of his Income per year, while Households were still saving almost Two months income per year; though the Consumption of Each was higher than ever. Real Tax impact on all remained fairly stable since the onset of World War II, with each Income level paying approximately their fair share; based on the total levels of Income for the Class, and percentage of tax paid on this total Income. Circumstances were about to change for the worse.

The United States, especially it's Government, had been profligate in the previous score of years. Military Procurement continued to increase due to the Cold War, though the level was at approximately 230% of need; solely generated by the Military/Industrial Complex. Infrastructure was expanded at a tremendous rate, with development of Interstate, National Parks and Dams, widespread Construction contracts for Military bases and missile silos, and development of modern airports. Much of this Infrastructure construction was financed by deficit spending or Bond issuance. Draft on Resources reached incredible levels, with an Inflationary spiral starting in Resource pricing.

The 1960s brought Kennedy to the White House, and a proposed Tax Cut to stimulate the Economy. Most Economists say this Tax Cut fueled the new Boom. This Author asserts it only fueled Inflation of a major venue. Individual Taxpayers remember this Keynesian Tax Cut not at all; it being only a two-shot spread of a few bucks in Rebate. The Corporations rejoice in this Tax Cut to this Day, which cut the real Tax impact they faced, by approximately One-third. The Wealthier classes also benefitted hugely, never again faced with as high a real Tax impact. The Tax Cut was supposed to offset the loss to the American Economy, of the re-establishment of the industries of the other Industrialized Nations-Europe and Japan. The Fallacy was soon apparent, as first Foreign Trade did not diminish; ever in Dollar terms, or adjusted for Inflation. The second element lay in the fact American Gross Domestic Product never altered in significant degree, from it's previous decade's rate of growth; when adjusted for Inflation.

The result of the Tax Cut brought a shift in real Tax impact to the lower income classes, a vast expansion of investment in paper financial instruments rather than real Capital investment, and a huge increase in Corporate profits. The expansion of the Economy brought a distorted increase in Resource prices, and rise in American purchase of foreign resources, especially Oil. The purchasing power of the American Worker started to erode, with the double whammy of a increased real Tax impact plus higher Consumer prices. The Government added to the problem by hiding the real reduced Tax base by Deficit Spending. The involvement in NATO and SEATO initially brought an effective American Occupation Army in Europe, which consumed any Foreign Trade surplus; and an Asian war financed by deficit spending, with a huge consumption of resources. The sum total of Government mis-allocations reduced the position of the average American household to it's position in 1940, by the year of 1970. This reality was hidden only by the entrance of American Women, read Wives, back into the American Labor force; from their leave-taking in the late 1940s. The gain of Ten years was it took Two laborers to generate the same standard of living; all due to erroneous Government Budget and Tax policy.

The Federal Government chose not to readjust real Tax impacts with the coming of the Vietnam War. The huge deficit spending thereby brought huge Corporate profits, which Management moved to maintain after the War. The movement towards Sector division of Corporations began, each division dictated to produce it's own Profit. The pressure to provide immunity from the IRS for these Profits also began. The Oil Embargo of 1973 made clear American dependence on Foreign resources. Oil Companies found greater Profits from the higher Prices, and forestalled Government efforts to reestablish American independence on Oil; a tendency which spread to other industries, interested in the higher Profits of higher Foreign resources pricing on the American domestic market. Native American industries, especially Coal and Steel, started their decline; while foreign consumer products began to seriously replace American products on the domestic market.

The Cotton Mills closed, as foreign manufacturers could produce cheaper than provision of a subsistence wage to American labor. Corporate Profits and Paper Financial Instrument Profits continued to soar untaxed, while American industry floundered.

The spread distortion of American Wealth began, with more and more of the American labor force dropping out of the Middle Class, and the Upper Classes gaining Equity, at least in Paper Profits. Government first attempted a Welfare program, hugely increasing the National Debt; later moving to purported Business incentive, without any attempt to change the real Tax impact. The Welfare programs added little economic incentive, as they did not provide a real improvement in Consumption patterns; though they did create the Era of Entitlements, the pattern where Government is forestalled from reducing most major expenditures.

The debacle of Medicare and Medicaid is a real case in point; Today, almost Everyone is guaranteed the same relative medical care as the highest Income earners. Workers cannot afford medical care with medical insurance beyond reach; and Medicare Supplement policies as high as total medical insurance premiums in 1965, the year Medicare was introduced. The cost of Medical care has increased by 14% per year since 1965; while the quality of Medical care increased by Three percent per year for the first Twenty years, then decreased by about a percentage point per year. The Business Incentive programs introduced with the Reagan administration signified nothing more than a furtherance of removal of real Tax impact from Corporations and the Wealthy Classes. The National Debt continued to balloon, and Profits increased in their Paper nature; without real increase in Economic productivity.

The first indication of real Economic failure came with the failure of the Banking system in the mid-1980s. Everyone conversant with the Period, knows about the Savings and Loans Bailout. Few recognize the Crisis was almost as bad for the Banks, but hidden by the swift action of the Federal Reserve System. The failure of the Banking system simply reflected the Paper nature of the Investment under the Reagan Tax Cut, which further distorted the real Tax impact upon the Wealthy, throwing the Tax burden on the Lower Classes. There were no real Profits in the Boom produced by Reagan's Tax Cut; and the Banking system failure expressed no real earnings from this Boom. The Consumption patterns of Workers, first eroded by the Kennedy Tax Cut, continued to erode at a substantive Two percent per year in real Product purchase; the Consumption pattern of Workers eroded at approximately Four percent per year after the Reagan Tax Cut. The American Economy deteriorated for a decade after the Reagan Tax Cut.

President Bush increased Taxes during his administration, but only against all Classes; his Tax program did not significantly alter the real Tax impact. The Economy received no real shot in the Arm, and the Standard of Living continued to decline; as Unemployment rose, and Factory Orders receded. The Balance of Trade had been developing a vast Deficit since the 1973 Oil Embargo. Poor Economic performance along with rapidly rising domestic purchase of foreign products because of their cheaper quality, brought huge erosion to the Dollar under the Bush administration. The United States found it hard to finance it's need of foreign resources, and it's higher-cost production with inferior quality lost a great share of Foreign Trade. Agricultural Sales alone saved the American Balance of Trade.

The American Turnaround came with the Clinton Tax Increase. The real element of this Tax Increase was the nature of the change of real Tax impact. The Working Classes were already overburdened with Taxes by 1993, and could not pay an effective higher percentage of their Income as Tax; though the Dollar value of their Taxes did go up. Corporations and Wealthy had Taxes reimposed by the Tax Increase. This increase of their real Tax impact was not a major alteration; basically only reinstating the taxes imposed before the Reagan Tax Cut. This forced assumption of an added share of Government expenditures did apply a real Economic stimulus. Working Class Consumption patterns immediately started to rise, as they were freed of a significant support of Government expenditures. A Boom was began, which eventually reversed the Deficit Spending of the Federal Government.

The National Debt started to decrease, and increasing burdens on the American Labor force were removed. The Economy started to rapidly expand, fueled by Consumer Demand; an item on which all Economists are agreed. Housing construction started to skyrocket. Consumers found their disposable income increasing faster than the Inflation rate; something unknown since the Kennedy Tax Cut. Aggregate American Household Wealth increased by approximately Two percent per year, between 1995 and 2000. The Unemployment rate dropped to a Low, no seen since World War II. The quality and durability of American products rose by an average of Three percent per year, after 1991; leading to a significant regain of Foreign trade for the American economy. More American Labor was entering the Middle Class, than falling to Lower Classes, after 1997; more Middle Class was entering the Upper Classes after 1995, than were entering the Middle Class from below. The total of American society resembled the mix of American society of the 1950s, by the year 1999. This was almost entirely due to removal of burden for Government expenditures from the Working Classes, to the Corporations and the Wealthy. The largesse of this burden removal was little more than $70 Billion in 1993. It had grown to $340 Billion by 1999. Clouds started to form on the Horizon.

Stock Options have been with Us, as long as the modern-style Corporation; their wide-scale use came only with the Reagan Tax Cut. Corporate Managements watched the vast reduction of Corporate taxes, and thought of methodology to personally share in the benefice. They chose the mechanism of Stock Options. Huge awards began to be bestowed on Corporate Executives, with the goal of absorbing the Tax savings as personal gain. The practice continued with the Years, and fortunes were made through the Stock Options venue by Corporate Management. The Clinton Tax Increase brought threat to this fortune-building endeavor. Corporate Management searched for methods to maintain the practice, which Corporate Stockholders would not notice, as loss of dividends.

Corporate Management focused on two avenues for the maintenance of Profits in the face of increased Taxation. They first examined the practice of Sector Accounting. The division of separate areas of Corporate production in Sectors, with separate Accounting and budgets, had begun in the 1960s; and the practice of forcing each Sector to present it's own Profits, had really begun with the 1970s. The Reagan administration allowed for the fiction these Profits were representative repayment for Capitalization by the overall Corporate organization; and non-taxable. Corporate Management, with the advent of the Clinton Tax Increase, thought to double, or triple, the profit ratios of these Sectors. They were helped in this by technological advance; with cheapened Product unit cost; which they only had to refuse to pass on to the Consumer as reduced Retail prices. This allowed for continued issuance of Stock Options, though not of the same magnitude as prior to the Clinton Tax Increase.

The second avenue adopted by multi-national Corporations was the hiding of Corporate payments in foreign accounts. Such payments could be claimed as not subject of American Corporate tax law. This venue became so exercised, many of the largest Corporations pay nothing in Corporate Income Tax—most notable Enron, Coca-Cola, etc. Even Corporations with almost no foreign Sales vastly reduce their Corporate tax, by having Retailers pay foreign subsidiaries. Real Corporate percentage tax having been dropping since the first impact of the Clinton Tax Increase.

The thirst for higher Profits to initiate Stock Options for Management has led to such In-line Production Profits-taking, it was starting to erode Consumer Demand by 1999; an effective reduction of real Tax impact on Corporations and the Wealthy Classes, again forcing the Working Classes to assume more of the tax burden. Stock Options increased the total number of Paper instruments existent; all demanding a high rate of return, for Corporate Management to exercise their

Stock Option with good Price. In-line Production Profits-taking continues to increase; now to produce the necessary dividends, as well as the Funds for further Stock Options. Consumers face higher Retail prices when lower Prices are dictated by cheaper means of Production. They also have to endure a greater share of the real Tax burden of Government expenditure. The Two above-mentioned avenues used by Corporate Management, means an evasion of Corporate Income Tax estimated at $400 Billion per year Today.

The Wealthy Classes in America have watched the American Economic Boom since 1993, and felt gladdened by the huge increase in their fortunes. They also witnessed the total rise in the Dollar value of their Capital Gains taxation, and groaned. The Wealthy applied pressure to their Congressional Representatives, to reduce the total Dollar value of their tax contributions. Congress has amended Capital Gains reportage every year since 1996, to reduce the total percentage actually paid as tax; this through spread over future years because of reinvestment. The effect is a real Tax impact reduction on the Wealthy Classes; an effective erosion of the Clinton Tax Increase.

The George W. Bush administration came into office, claiming it would undo the inequities of heavy taxation. The tax burden on Americans, prior to the Bush Tax Cut, was only approximately Eighty percent of the Clinton Tax Increase; a real tax reduction of Twenty percent, during the Clinton Presidency. The real element of the Bush Tax Cut results in the reduction of the real Tax impact on Corporations and the Wealthier Classes, to a point lower than the real Tax impacts upon them after the Reagan Tax Cut.

The Bush administration already proposes a Government Spending Deficit equivalent to the level of Deficits during his Father's administration. Republicans claim this is on account of the Terrorist attacks. The Economic fact will be seen with at least a doubling of the Deficit level claimed, due to a loss of Tax revenues under the Tax Cut. There are already signs of a loss of Consumer Demand, destroying current favorable Economic Indicators. A continued softening of Consumer

Demand will present even greater losses of Tax Revenue. George W. Bush may remind his Father of John Quincy Adams; he resembles Herbert Hoover to this Author.

It is clear from this Chapter's outline that Government Tax Policy remains the major propellent, or deterrent, of the American Economy. Monetarist Economic Policy stands as a minor influence with the presence of a modern Banking system; solely concerned with the effective management of the Banking system itself. Equally clear stands the fact Congress and President follow a format specifically outlined to benefit their own Class of Wealth. Working Classes face an increased real Tax impact under the new Tax Cut, whether this is represented through higher taxes; or through the practice of Deficit spending. The Author can say with confidence rigid reintroduction of the Clinton Tax Increase with it's real increase of real Tax impact upon Corporation and the Wealthy Classes, would avoid Deficit spending. Reversion to the Tax Code existent (real Tax impact rates, not necessarily nominal rates) before the Kennedy Tax Cut would guarantee a Boom equivalent to the late 1990s for another decade.

3

Entitlements and COLAs

The lexicon brought forward from the 1970s ties the hands of Today's Government. Individuals, under any Government, do possess certain guarantees of protection—for personal safety and protection of private property. Entitlements, though, establish a permanent gain to which an Individual claims title. The basic surmise states once an Individual effects some bounty from the Government; the grant is forwarded perpetually throughout his life. Temporary need becomes permanent Windfall. The Government's hands are tied; the Courts insisting upon maintenance of the stipends.

The greatest example, which will anger every Veteran, comes with the examination of Military disabilities. Over Eight percent of the ex-Veterans who have become multi-millionaires since their exit from the Service, still draw their disabilities' checks. This Disabilities system was set up by the Military so wounded Veterans who had lost the full physical capability to work at gainful employment, could have their expenses and lowered income offset by monthly allotment. In excess of Eighty percent of the Disabled Veterans drawing monthly disability checks Today, do so with incomes equivalent to their Peers in Occupation and Society. This Author understands the debt We owe to Our Veterans; but the system of military disabilities as organized, simply provides these Veterans with back-pay on their military service, which their unwounded Comrades are not allowed to draw. Many of these unwounded Comrades drew scant pay for their service—often less than

$100 per month; while their wounded-in-service friends can now compute their service pay in Thousands of dollars per month of Service. The inequity of the system can be seen. This rationale does not desire to eliminate military disabilities, or injure the standard of living of those Veterans suffering loss of Income from disabilities deriving from military service to this Country; it is a simple statement asserting all disability payments should be based upon need, no matter how acquired.

The Social Security system amplifies the great need for change in Government procedure. The current system operates upon a point-system, where the amount a Worker has paid in determines the level of benefit. The common defense of this system lies in a claim it is the only way to protect individual property rights, and to forestall a Wealth redistribution plan. Economist and Policy-maker ignore the realities of modern life. The introduction of Medicare, along with maximum limits being placed upon the Income paid; assured the Social Security system would not protect property rights, and turned the System into a Wealth redistribution system.

Medicare was set up originally to help Seniors defray extreme costs of Medical care. It quickly turned into a system to insure all Recipients could acquire the best Medical care available, previously available only to those who could afford. The cost of Medical Care immediately skyrocketed, with Doctors allowed to charge as highly as any other Doctor in the Country. The design of Medicaid opened this best Medical care to the Poor as well. A ten Dollar visit to the Doctor in 1965 has turned into a average $85 visit to a Doctor's clinic Today. It is very fortunate for the Patient, if the added pay buys more than Ten minutes of the Doctor's personal time. Additional time spent by the Doctor on a Patient comes only with greatly accelerated rates of pay. Government intervention in medical payment schedules obviously introduced a massive inflation rate into those schedules.

The Caps placed on the amount of Social Security deductions allowed in dollar amounts, altered the previous formulation of the

Social Security benefit allocation system. The Caps assure not Recipient will ever pay for the entirety of the benefits received, because of the inflated medical costs under the Medicare addition. The average level of benefits, plus the average medical costs of the Senior, will always exceed the amount previously paid into the system by the Recipient. The Social Security System has become a Wealth redistribution system, with Wealth being transferred from the Young to the Elderly. Many derivations can be drawn from the above fact.   The separation of monthly allotments based on the amounts paid in by the Individual no longer holds validity. The lower Incomes which paid in less, obviously do not pay their fair share. The upper Incomes, with Caps on the taxable income under which Social Security deductions apply, also do not pay their fair share; with the advent of Medicare. It is clear those who have lower monthly allotments under the system, could use higher allotments; because their level of Income had always been lower. Equally apparent stands the fact those who draw higher monthly allotments, need those allotments less than those who draw less, because of original higher Incomes.

The rationale of the Social Security system has changed; from Everyone drawing from the system according to what they have paid in, to a format where although no One pays their fair share, some draw higher because they cost less than others. This immediately brings need to examine the different allotment scales, to discern just what differentials of Cost exist. An amazing fact comes to light. Those paid the higher monthly allotments actually cost the system more, because the allotment increases are much more expensive than the rising Medical costs, due to the total dollars amounts involved continued repetitively. The lower monthly allotment Recipients cost the Social Security system less, than do the higher allotment Recipients. Not only has the Social Security system become a Wealth redistribution system; but the Wealthier Recipients, determined by their higher monthly allotments, receive the great Wealth redistribution. They get the full Medical costs made by Medicare, which exceed the amounts paid in by all; but they receive much higher monthly allotments.

The current system does not protect individual property rights, the Young are being victimized. It does not forestall Wealth redistribution; the lower Income Poor must redistribute their Wealth to the Elderly along with the higher Income Youth, but the greatest beneficiaries of this Wealth redistribution are the higher allotment Recipients. The result is a Wealth Redistribution which should please the Wealthy; take from the Poor, and give it to the Wealthy. The Social Security system, as existent Today, constitutes a regressive tax upon the Poor. This process, itself, must be examined with the eyes of the Economist.

The Medicare system turned the Social Security System into a Wealth redistribution system; but also vastly inflated Medical costs. Medical personnel universally belong to the wealthier classes, being specialized professionals. Medicare can be assumed to have doubled their Income, and tripled their business. Wealthier individuals hold far greater Stock, than do poorer people. Medicare vastly increased the Profits of Medical Provider Companies and Institutions. It can be assumed Medicare payments doubled the Profits of these Companies, leading to a total dollar enrichment of Stock dividends. Examination of the process in detail concludes Medicare increased the Equity of the Wealthier classes by at least Fifteen percent of the Total Wealth of these Classes; through simple multiplied Medical costs. This alone was an extreme regressive tax upon the Working classes.

Social Security monthly allotments today range from $400-1800. Estimated funds needed for living assistance stand at about One Thousand dollars per month, when considering Rent, Food, Clothing, and Intermediate Product renewal. Close to half of the monthly allotment issued remain less than $1000 per month. The Seniors receiving these allotments could not subsist, without input of additional resources; provided by themselves or additional assistance. Close to Thirty percent of monthly allotments issued by Social Security are for amounts in excess of $1100 per month. Eliminating all allotments over $1000 per month could pay for at least Seventy percent of the Cost of raising all allotments to $1000 per month.

The introduction of a uniform Allotment in the Social Security system, based upon the living assistance needs of Recipients, would cost little more in the long-run than does the current system; it would also raise the living standard of Seniors greatly, provide almost a Four percent increase in Consumer Demand, and eliminate much of the regressive taxation on the Young. This regressive reduction comes through a more positive Wealth redistribution, eventual inheritance of the less-spent assets of the Elderly, and greater stability to the Social Security system itself through reduced Accounting procedures and less Employment.

This Author previously expounded on the Medicare system itself (Plans for the Future, Xlibris, 2000). Congress needs to alter the operating procedure of Medicare. The basic premise of the operating procedure must stand on subsistence care. Medicare was enabled to provide basic subsistence care for the Elderly, followed by Medicaid for the Poor. The Social Security administration altered this Mandate, moving to a position of underwriting any medically-proven procedure, which provided possibility for the lengthening of life. The Social Security administration is currently considering underwriting Organ transplants. The entire direction of Medical research threatens to quadruple medical costs. The Social Security administration plans to underwrite these costs. These plans threaten the viability of the Social Security System itself.

The provision of subsistence care gives basic medical care for all Recipients. They are guaranteed basic medical procedures, basic medical services, basic levels of medical attention, and basic necessary medications. High-Cost medical procedures would be uniformly turned down; cutting Forty percent of the operating costs of Medicare. It is not to deny high-cost medical procedures from Recipients; but such medical procedures must be paid by Insurance, State assistance, or Case-by-Case special underwriting from separate Federal grants. It will be plainly seen by all Readers this reduction to subsistence care for the Social Security system means a rise in Medical insurance premiums, reduction of the number of high-cost medical procedures conducted, and resort to these high-cost medical procedures only when there is high viability of Patient Recovery to normal life. The end-result will be a lessening of the medical costs in this Country, on a per-Patient basis.

The discussion to this point alienates most Readers; yet, they must accustom themselves to the realities of life. Medical statistics themselves express the limitations of these high-cost medical procedures. Every such medical procedure has a viability chart; Seventy percent of all medical Patients possible to be helped, will gain no benefit by the procedure, due to additional medical problems. Twenty percent of such Patients will only delay the inevitability of death by the medical procedure, simply delaying the onset with much suffering and cost. Ten percent may be assumed to gain some long-term benefit from the medical procedure. It stands as obvious medical procedures which only magnify medical costs, without some return to normalcy for the Patient; are in the interest of no One, except the Profits picture of Medical Providers.

The nature of Congress will provide extraordinary funds for indigent high-cost medical service provision. This provision will be on a Case-by-Case basis, if left entirely outside of the standard Social Security system; this because these medical decisions are the sole basis of their empowerment, with no stipulation for overall Patient care. Patients will be treated fairly based upon their physical ability to benefit from such high-cost medical procedures. Almost half of these procedures will be paid by private medical insurers. The cost of these medical procedures will go down, as the lessened number of procedures conducted will reduce the number of facilities maintained for these procedures. The remaining facilities will become specialized, and provide for the majority of these procedures. The specialization assure the procedures will be conducted with the highest professional skill. The down-the-road Cost for Government will be Twenty percent the expense of the current system.

Return to the above discussion shows Wealth redistribution curtailed by the above recommendations. Reversion to subsistence care for the Social Security system brings additional benefits. The limitations of care offered, allows the Social Security system to introduce Quality Control to the system. Medicare does not worry about medical technique, or the evolution of Medicine; they will only be concerned with the quality of basic services provided. Uniform standards of care and compliance can be demanded; and Investigators trained easily to the level of quality surveillance. The Controls implemented can assure a much higher quality of basic medical care. The Medicare program becomes a lower medical review board of correct medical practice.

The downside of medical provision under the new system will be a lowered Life Expectancy in this Country; but most medical authorities would not expect a drop of more than Three or Four years. The provision of quality basis subsistence medical care would mean the suffering endured by medical patients would reduce at least Fifty percent, maybe more; due to the elimination of extreme measures to prolong life. Those who have a chance, will get that chance; those who don't have a chance, will be allowed to die with dignity, and without suffering intense tortures. One often has to be cold, to be kind!

The methodology of Medicare premiums and deductibles remain a nightmare of paper, for no valuable cause. Congress demands premiums as excuse for the program, and assert deductibles forestall unnecessary use of the Medicare system. Private HMOs provide an advance guard solution to the issue of premiums. Many adopt a co-payment system where a set fee is paid at the Health Provider. Medicare should have assumed such a program from the start. Seniors require vigilant medical attention to preserve health. This insists on significant yearly visits which mandate the use of the deductible in full; the deductible thereby does not limit unnecessary medical use of the Medicare system, it actually increases this unnecessary use as Seniors attempt to get medical care before the end of the year with renewal of deductible. Premium and deductible should be paid proportionably per visit, and at the health provider site. A co-payment charge of $20-50 per visit could be charged.

Analysis of this co-payment Medicare system brings light to real benefits. The co-payment charge would immediately deter unnecessary visits, because it must be paid at health provider site at the time of the visit. The charge would be low, so deterrence of visit when this visit is medically necessary, remains irrelevant. Medicare premium payment and deductible will be paid with actual use, so Seniors of low Income are not victimized. Medicare benefits are not paid by either premiums or deductibles at present, so loss of universal payment per year will increase Medicare expense only marginally for the Labor force—possibly up to $50 Billion per year. The co-payment system of set charge allows for open-end levels of premium and deductible payment by actual users of the Medicare system; while a program of reimbursement for low Income disadvantaged over a certain limit, can be introduced. Accounting procedures of Medicare could be simplified; the set charge deducted from any bill to any Medicare recipient, from any health provider. The health providers realize they must collect the co-payment, else face it's loss to themselves. Medicare Recipients need only be notified of the extent of the rest of their co-payment under the Medicare regulations. This furthers medical assistance for Seniors in very important ways.

Most Seniors become terrified with the complexity of medical Accounting procedures. Almost all share some loss of Sight, plus Medicare billings use small print and confusing regulations. Medicare Supplement health insurers use even smaller print and more confusing regulations. Seniors often retire to realize their own medical care will prove to be a more complex business, than the occupation they previously enjoyed. Their Age and loss of mental acuity assure they can never fully comprehend the information which descends upon them. Their inabilities to complete all expected of them; cause almost $3 Billion per year loss through added mailings and lost payments. The co-payment system for Medicare could almost eliminate Seniors' participation in the medical Accounting system. Medicare Supplement Health Insurers could be mandated to pay Medicare what they will pay on assigned medical bills of Seniors, with Medicare paying the Health Providers both their payment plus the Medicare Supplement payment; the Health Providers then billing the Medicare Recipient once, for the entire amount owed. This leaves the entire Medicare medical Accounting procedure in the hands of trained Accounting personnel, until a Bill, comprehendible to Seniors, is sent for payment.

Economic analysis of the above proposals provide possible economic benefits of the above initiatives. The reduction of Medicare to subsistence care reduces the Medicare bill to Taxpayers by $200-400 Billion dollars per year. A replacement program for provision of High-Cost medical procedures would likely cost between $100-200 Billion per year for American Taxpayers. Medicare Supplement Health Insurers would reduce their payments by $50 Billion per year, with possible total reduction in health premiums. The introduction of the proposed Co-payment at site system would cost a potential $30 Billion per year, due to the loss of universal premium and deductibles payment. This could be offset completely, and a gain introduced; as the set co-payment advanced to $50 per Visit. The reduction of Accounting Costs for Medicare and Medicare Health Insurers could mean up to $10 Billion per year in savings, due to timely payments and reduced Accounting hours of labor. An adoption of a standard, uniform monthly allotment could mean an increased payment of $20 Billion per year initially; but with the retirement of the Baby Boomers, could accomplish Savings of up to $100 Billion per year. Now is the time to make changes in the Social Security system.

The process of COLAs present a source of greater Conflict. Cost of Living Advances theory stands upon the protection of People, who are on set Incomes; from the destructive power of Inflation. They have altered in nature greatly, since their initial use. Their use has been applied to Incomes, which do not meet the criteria of Set Income. This practice brings alteration to the basic Wage—scale format, and in ways which promote inequities of Income.

Set Incomes must be defined as those Incomes which do not fluctuate at comparable rate, with what Economists sometimes call 'Released Incomes'. Released Incomes enjoy Power in the Marketplace, with a demanded higher return in the face of rising Costs; most generally by the provision of Goods or Services. Set Incomes do not contain this Power, either through legal contract or set Equity. Cost of Living Advances operate differently, depending on if they underwrite Set Incomes, or Released Incomes.

Cost of Living Advances provision for Released Incomes actually set up a Price/Wage schedule of Wage Increase. The Procedure installs an automatic Wage increase, in lieu of Wage bargaining procedures. A boon to Labor as seen by most; it is equally a boon to Business, allowing for automatic Product Price increases. Released Incomes are relieved of the threat of service-value review; where Labor or Service finds itself in a new Wage/Value schedule. The Released Incomes get the Wage increase, whether their Productivity has gained or lost in value. This immunity from reevaluation insures automatic further Inflation, because Wage scales remain improperly set. The Market system of setting Costs and Prices stands circumvented; Prices reflect an artificial height, because of enhanced Costs without justification.

Set Incomes, on the other hand, present a distinct Scenario, from the action of COLAs upon Released Incomes. Set Incomes represent a direct reduction in Household and Income consumption, because of insufficient funds. There exists no alternative, except to reduce Purchase. This loss of consumption means a lowering of the Standard of Living for the Set Income households, and a loss of Production to the total Economy. Costs of Living Advances to Set Incomes insures a set level of consumption by these households; a betterment of their lifestyle and Economic production. Economic studies indicate COLAs on Set Incomes produce relatively no or light Price increases; primarily because of full labor usage of the Retail sector, and economies of fuller Production (higher Capital equipment use).

Lumping the delivery of COLAs to Released Incomes and Set Incomes together, with equal economic impact; omits the impact of over-evaluation of Released Income labor. The Production schedule is skewed upward to higher Cost, and Market demand reduces in response. Relative Production reduces in magnitude, because of loss of Sales. COLAs for Set Incomes operate as an economic incentive; COLAs for Released Incomes produce economic disincentive. The separation point existing exactly where arbitration can be utilized to readjust Income.

The mechanical operation of Cost of Living Advances promotes inequity. COLAs operating through Set Incomes germinate far less inequity, than those operating through Released Incomes. These Incomes generally share a magnitude three times that of Set Income. A percentage Cost of Living Advance will always benefit higher Incomes more than lower Incomes. Set Incomes predictably need endure three times the Inflation, to get the same nominal benefit as Released Incomes. Their endurance of this level of Income signifies only the Released Incomes will still receive three times the nominal benefit. A percentage operation of COLAs means the inequity of Income will be maintained, with Released Incomes of higher magnitude enjoying much greater flexibility of purchase; enduring the process of Inflation.

Released Incomes and Employers also use Cost of Living Advances as automatic Wage raises. Promotional levels are set whereby Labor is assured increases in promotional Wages, during the period of their understudy. Negotiation of Wage increases become structured, so Labor can understand the level of personal income through the process of employment, and judge the relative time of his promotions to new Wage grades. Employers can establish stable Wage/Cost schedules for future Production. This actually integrates automatic Price increases of Product production; leaving only avenues of Layoffs, if Production schedules are not met. This is forced freeze of Market forces, in the determination of Costs of Production.

The Federal Government holds the title, as worst offender of Wage schedule negotiations; though State and Local Government stand close with the Federal Government. The Federal Civil Service, as organized Today, holds all the horrors any Employer could face; a total inability of Employer to fire, Employer restriction from reducing Manpower complement by department or task, forced promotion based upon simple seniority, automatic pay raises in grade by seniority, regulated rates of labor effort, inability of Employer to schedule efficient Work times, and Court-ordered un-rescindable benefits. Firing Employees requires an arbitration process so complex; it is easier and far cheaper to tell the Employee to stays home, and pay the Individual through the rest of his Thirty Year employment, if this Employee can be convinced to retire. The system holds such immunity, policy changes cannot be effected in work procedures; throughout several administrations interested in the same change.

Federal Civil Service regulations insure the Federal Budget will expand almost Two percent per year, simply to fulfil Wage increases and built-in COLAs. An un-nerving aspect of Federal employment resides in the fact new policies require new Civil Service hires, because Management cannot transfer labor elements out of older, defunct departments. These new Hires immediately attain all the protections of their older brethren. Occupations, or labor duties, cannot be altered without the consent of the employed; most often, it requires promotion and raise to get them to retrain for other duties. The last this Author has heard, there were still Seven Switchboard Operators at Capital Hill; though Congress went Direct Dial in 1963.

A reversion to discussion of the Federal Budget necessitates comment stipulating Civil Service regulations must be altered, in order for the growth of the Federal Budget to be stopped. Legislation must be passed, which must endure the Courts; to dismiss Civil Servants in the interest of the Government. This Law probably will require 'Buyouts'

of Employee rights, to satisfy the Courts. It will probably cost somewhere around Ten Billion dollars per year, for three or four years. It
will probably save Twenty Billion dollars per year, a decade down the
Road. Almost every Federal Department and Agency would utilize
such a Law if funded, to eliminate approximately Twenty percent of
it's labor complement. It is a very serious recommendation!

Entitlements and COLAs cost the Federal Government at least
$400 Billion per year, by even the most conservative estimate. Effective
alteration of these Two programs could easily shave off in excess of $80
Billion per year off this Cost. This could be done, without substantive
reduction of the protection of the Individuals concerned in the system.
The Problem consists solely in finding the effective alternatives, for
achievement of this Goal. The discussion below highlights many of the
issues.

The first element of the Problem belongs to the enablement of the
Civil Service, especially it's Civil Service Commission. The entirety of
the Agency acts, and is treated like, a Federal department of the Government. The Civil Service Commission serves as both Regulator of
and Advocate for Civil Service Employees. It's position as Regulator is
compromised, as Civil Service Commission members and staff are
themselves Civil Servants; also affected by all regulations set up and
enforced. It's advocacy for Civil Service Employees stand curtailed, as
they must act as Management supervision of these Employees, under
their Empowerment by Congress. This resolves into two Jobs, which
are in direct conflict with each other.

Congressional empowerment of the Civil Service must be altered,
turning the Civil Service into a Government-sanctioned Union of
Employees. The Civil Service Commission should be eliminated, in
favor of a Joint Congressional Committee of Governmental Employment. This Joint Committee need hire Congressional aides empowered
to negotiate with the new Union, on matters of Wages, Benefits, and
Retirement Funding. The Civil Service Union would elect Union offi-

cials and Benefits Negotiators. Real alteration of Employment structure can be accomplished with this done.

The first Congressional Act past this point, must be enabled Contract of Labor Services. Employees would not be granted permanent employment; deriving only Contractual employment of specified duration—suggest Three or Five Year Contracts. All Wage, Benefits, and Retirement funding would be stipulated in the Contract, for the full period in question. The Congressional Act forbids further contractual negotiations for the duration of the Contract. The Employment Contracts will not have universal Wage and Benefits packages per Occupational grade; but will be based on the Cost of Living in the State or Region contracted for. Employee transfer cannot be conducted, without negotiation of a new Employment Contract. Employment Contracts can be terminated by the Government with Three months notice, upon judgement of inferior performance of Three levels of Supervision. Employment can be terminated by the Employee, based upon his belief of discrimination in employment opportunity or Workplace environment; in neither case, can Compensation be granted to the Employee for such discrimination, unless the Employee can prove Criminal violation of his Rights in a Federal Court.

Civil Service employment will not be contiguous, dependent upon renewal of negotiated Contracts of stipulated duration. Employees will be constrained by Law, from attempting Wage or Benefit negotiation on previously-signed Contracts. The Congressional aides negotiating for the Government, will not be Civil Servants themselves; they will be contracted Regional aides, who compete for Negotiation Contracts with Congress. They undoubtedly will begin their careers as current Employment agencies; their conduct in negotiations monitored by the Joint Congressional Committee and Congressional Staff. The Civil Service Union will be empowered to report abuses in the negotiation of Employment Contracts, to the Joint Congressional Committee.

The value of the above Negotiation process lies in the gradual descent of Wage and Benefits packages granted to Civil Service employees, to those levels consistent with the Region of employment. The cost of the Congressional contracted Negotiators should only marginally exceed current rates charged by Employment Agencies at present; though the Federal Government will undoubtedly have to pay the Charges, rather than the Employee, as in Private employment. The refusal of re-negotiation of older Contracts of limited duration, insures elimination of heavy pressure for more Benefits or Wage increases; the Employee being faced with possible legal termination, when future negotiations take place. The need for qualified Labor will insure employment standards meet Community standards of the Region.

The Author has previously suggested a Draft, or Conscription, for Civil Service as well as Military Service. The above suggestion grants much of the same benefit as a Conscription; but also providing higher continuity and closer alignment with American values. Management Specialists will assert the negotiation process brings great disruption to Labor effort; but it is a lie, as proven by Private industry performance. They have used Personal Employment Contracts with great success, for many years. The limited-duration Employment Contracts allow Supervisory personnel to inform Employment Contractors, if they desire to retain their current help; or if they find the difficulty of re-training the lesser of two evils. Civil Service employment would descend to equivalence with Private employment, responding to the same Economic forces. The drain of Skills between the Public and Private Sectors would cease; while transfer of necessary skills could be accomplished, with competition between Private and Public sectors. Government Retirement packages would become less excessive, while Private Sector Retirement packages would become more generous; in the competition process, generated by the need for skilled labor. Government would without doubt benefit from lower Labor Costs, than visible under the current structure.

The combination of Employment Buyouts, negotiating limited-duration Employment Contract, and Grand-fathering Retirement could revamp the Federal Civil Service successfully within a short

period (potential one Presidential administration). The only requirements for this process is a resolute Congress, and a dedicated President.
This altered state would also possess an additional benefit of administration: the entrenched resistence to policy change could be vastly
reduced. The Program outlined above serves equally well for elimination of opposition to Policies, originating in the ranks of the Civil Service. Both Congress and President would benefit from this advantage;
while American Taxpayers witness a reduction of Budget burden.

A introduction of a uniform Social Security monthly benefit for
Seniors brings a possibility of relieving the final vestiges of Cost of Living Advances' injury. Elimination of the percentage COLA could be
accomplished, thereby eliminating the advantage gain of scale of
Income; through taking a percentage COLA of the uniform benefit
alone, as it can be claimed as Living Subsistence Standard. This determined nominal amount could stand as the sole increase for all
COLAs—whether to Set Incomes, or Released Incomes. This guarantees a removal of extensive Inflationary pressure from the issuances of
COLA increases. It further grants the American Taxpayers a $3 Billion
saving in the Federal Budget alone, at a minimum—which increases
every year in size. The actual loss of Consumer demand would be nil,
while actual Consumption would increase.

The Author treads 'Hallowed Ground' with his next proposal. His
contention states United States Military forces presents the greatest
under-utilized labor force existent in this Country today. They could
serve as a highly-skilled, trained labor force to Private industry, under
the correct circumstances. Truth actually decrees the Military has use
for only half their labor, outside of War conditions. The Military also
has need for more MOS-trained personnel under War conditions, than
it can effectively employ now. It remains the bane of all Peacetime military forces; change to War status demand a huge Force-complement
increase. The Author will present a Plan, which could alter the complexity of the situation, while decreasing the demand upon the Budget.

Domestic-based military troops present a Fifty percent under-utilization of labor, but in an Scenario where MOS-Complement stands as scant for National Defense. A Program should be introduced where Service troops serve only Six months of any Year in Domestic bases, though their pay would be extended like Teachers through the full Twelve Months. Relieved Troops could find alternate employment for the other Six Months, with half of the Troops on duty at any given Period. Domestic military installations would be allowed Twelve Thousand full-time serving Officers, and Thirty Thousand full-time serving NCOs. Military training programs could be fully utilized throughout the Year, rather than the Sixty percent utilization rate now current. Military pay could be reduced to Sixty-five percent of current MOS rates, and full training schedules could increase the numbers of trained personnel. American Taxpayers would actually face an increase in military expense in the Budget, but functionally increase the trained military cadres with only marginal increase of expense. The Economy would gain by the introduction of trained labor, into several areas of skilled-labor shortage.

The Budget finds many areas of gain from such alteration. The potential greatest long-term gain lay in the provision of Military retirements. The fact of the matter sits most military personnel would be serving only half the Quarters as previously, at Sixty-five percent of the pay. The higher rate of pay, plus the Quarters worked for Private enterprise, allow Government refusal of more than half of the current Retirement percentages of Pay. Government can even insist Private retirement plans bear their share of the medical costs of Retired Veterans. Staff requirements of the domestic Force structure can be minimized, with understanding these MOS positions are the highest Paygrades in the Service. Savings on such Retirements are therefore significantly higher. The higher Wage scales of Private employment will draw many of the older military personnel to retain their part-time employment, through expansion of it into full-time employment. This drift of older military personnel into the Private Sector, will reduce the actual

Retirement benefits to be paid; it also provides for a younger, qualified Reaction Force, willing to deploy faster because of less commitments. Demands for increases in military pay will decline, as lower-ranked military personnel begin to enjoy the advantages of Private employment. Economic expectation would suggest a potential reduction of $40 Billion per year from the Military aspect of the Budget, after an introductory Five year period.

Another annoying proposal for the Military comes in the suggestion all military troops be cross-trained as a Police force. This extends beyond Riot Control; with the full integration of Police procedure being introduced. This aspect increases the number of potential Police officers, who could be retained by local Authorities as Reserve officers; while increasing employment opportunities for military ranks, with unsuitable MOS qualifications for Private employment. The Military could establish an Employment Service for military personnel going off their Six months of active service; the Employment Service could maintain standing Contracts with the Custom Service, Border Service, and Secret Service. This Service could also establish Contracts for Airport Security, Train Security, provision of Security personnel for State Patrol forces, and provide security for Federal buildings and nuclear power plants. This suggestion will find a lot of resistance in the military establishment, who will not wish to expand beyond running through fields with a rifle. The Federal Employment Buyout program should also include military personnel.

The above Chapter hopefully goes great distance, in the discussion of elimination of impact of Entitlement and Cost of Living Advances to the Federal Budget. Similar analysis applies equally well to study of State and Local Budgeting. The real problem of Budget restraint comes from Politicians' lack of desire for the alienation of any segment of the Voting population. Civil Service, to Politicians, possesses real Terror; Civil Servants and their families have a Voting record some Forty percent higher than the national average, and they consistently vote for their own interests. Seniors, especially those with above-normal Social

Security monthly allotments, also share similarity with Civil Servants; they vote higher than the national average, and vote their own interest consistently. The major problem every Economist faces; lies in the presentation of a Economic model with enough benefit, that Politicians will risk the wrath of Voters. It is not sufficient to be right!.

4

Dispersal Analysis

The Federal Government exists as the greatest monstrosity ever imagined by Mankind. Someone once told the Author all departments and Agencies of the Federal Government could be listed on 87 pages, if the type and 4-column style of a Dictionary were used. The Author held disbelief in the statement; it was not enough space, and Computer listing remains only as good as the input into it. There are still Three operating military installations which have not met the Computer. Some funded Agencies probably have not been listed on Computer as yet; with Programers lacking knowledge of their existence. A check has not been made in years; but as late as 1980, there was still a funded Commission for Spanish-American War Veterans. A Commission for Dependents of Civil War Veterans was funded, as late as 1965. There are still Commissions funded for Public Housing Projects torn down in the 1970s. There are still funded Appropriations Committees for military bases closed some time ago. Public Library Commissions possess Federal budgeted funds, even though there are no registered membership on the Commissions, with the Libraries themselves torn down. Many D.C. sites have two Federal budget appropriations assigned; one for the building presently on site, one for the building previously torn down on that site. Commentary need not be made as to question where the Funds are going; it is sufficient to state many of these departments and Committees are not on Computer, though they find their way into current Budget proposals.

Anyone accessing any part of the Federal Government knows the Federal Government has forms for any type of informational minutia, but it still lacks unitary documentation for the budgetary process. Almost all Agencies, Departments, and Commissions devise their own form of Budget Proposal, specifically designed to hide undesirable results, and promote self-designed levels of appropriation. Congress, or more realistically, Congressional staffs find themselves confronted by thousands of budget proposals; all designed in deceptive formats differing one from another. These Congressional staffs content themselves with attempting to verify the data discernable in the documents, without grasp of any ratio alignment of numeral data left unspecified. The breakdown of numeral data in these Budget Proposals are remarked scant, with lowest-level data descending only to Millions of Dollars. Sub-departments of several thousand employees often get only a specified budgeting amount assigned, not even stipulating how it will be spent. Private Sector industries would shut down entire Plant operations, if faced with such a Budget Proposal; possessing no activity data, and not specifying desirable accomplishments.

Neither State or Defense Departments could come up with specific numbers of Individuals employed in each General Service Grade some years back. Such numeral-driven Organizations could not come up with statistical data about their own Table of Organization. The Defense Department, upon Presidential request, could not advance the number of currently-running sub-budgets in it's organization. The Department of the Interior cannot give number to the number of standing Commissions and Committee operating. The Justice Department cannot number the investigations currently underway, or tell the number the Investigators involved; though they can claim to be Eighteen percent understaffed. The Federal Bureau of Investigation can number their Employees, but cannot pinpoint their locations, work schedules, or current assignments. The U.S. Military does not known how many of it's personnel are on Leave, at any given point in time.

The Postal Service has the best record of Employee accounting of any Federal entity, if that can be believed.

This Swamp cannot be rationalized, without alteration of the basic Accounting practices now used. The most basic Accounting principle which must be introduced, must be a Computer program to match salary checks to a listed Table of Organization. Federal Departments, Agencies, and Commissions who cannot come up with such a Table of Organization; will have Employees unpaid. Congress should immediately pass legislation with precluding the Treasury from issuing salary checks to Any, not on a Table of Organization filed with the Treasury. A saving of a minimum of a Billion dollars per year could be attained by such measure.

Congress could reach further, and demand they be supplied with a like Table of Organization; which in addition, lists Work location, activity engaged upon, and normal Work schedule. Demand for total Work location areas, along with the hours said location operates, need be made; so Work schedules can be verified. Business leadership can inform these are basic Accounting procedures necessary to guaranteeing Employee fulfillment of Employment conditions. Congress probably do best, by turning this information over to Private Accounting agencies; who have shown far greater success over Civil Service, in maintaining such Accounting procedures. This alone will save $3 Billion per year from the Federal Budget.

Congress should employ Personal Credit Verification agencies to ascertain the truth of operating Work locations, filed in the Table of Organizations. These agencies could verify operation of the locations, like they do Individuals' personal credit history; talking to local businesses, local banks, and local law enforcement agents. This process may eliminate thousands of bogus locations; and if not, present Congress with a precise idea of where to close down excess Federal Work location areas. Federal Departments, Agencies, and Commissions often have Twenty-Thirty Work locations per major City, which could be reduced to Four or Five; set locations already possessing the Work space capacity. This concentration of Federal activity could cut Federal building maintenance and Construction costs, by as much as $10 Billion per year.

The above-mentioned venues are simple exercises, which any normal Private business would enter into; because of the automatic savings engendered. Government operation requires a different focus than Private business; yet, Accounting procedures for organizational structure remain relatively constant. Congress and President suffer from a general lack of control of the Executive branch of Government. This loss of control comes from the failure to implement basic Accounting and Responsibility procedures. The process need not create a new bureaucracy; effective use of Private Accounting and Security firms, along with proper dismissal procedures; could re-establish control. The gain for American Taxpayers might possibly reach a total of $100 Billion per year—when considering reduced Employment, reduced Benefits and Retirement payments, and reduction of immediate operating expenses.

The nexus of expanding Budget and incompetent Government appropriation combines at the point of Budget development. Private business operates on the principle of Profitability; with planning done at the Top, and Operating budgets set for department based upon desired Profit. Departments are ordered to operate inside their budgets, however it need be done. Department Supervisors realize they must perform within budget limits, or be replaced. It remains their responsibility for productivity and performance, within the parameters set.

The Federal Budgeting process operates in almost the exact opposite manner. Budget season opens when Management orders lowest budget elements to submit Budget proposals; this could basically be called 'Submit the Wish List'. The lowest environs devise everything they would like to get; then add Ten percent to the total, in fear of Congressional budget-cutting. Secondary level budget Management receive these Proposals, cut Ten percent, then add Five percent for their own discretionary funds. The third level and up (generally about Eight levels), get Secondary Budget Proposals, add Five percent for their own discretionary funds, and pass their Proposals up. The final proposed Budget presented to Congress exceeds the Bottom Wish List by about Forty percent; while in addition, containing another Twenty percent in actual intermediate-level expenses. Congressional staff now are prepared to consider the Budget Proposals.

Congressional staff possess absolutely no verification investigative powers. Their basic function is number-crunching for Congress. They start to add the numbers, and start to make suggestions to Congress; based not upon actual checked data, only on residual rounded numbers. Their suggestions typically suggest only methods to draw funds off some Budget Proposals, to gain funds for Congressional desires. They can accomplish this with confidence; knowing the Budget Proposals exceed actual needs for all departments. Congress remain the Front, never examining the Budget Proposals themselves which they could not understand; simply working off the numbers supplied by Congressional staff.

Congress' search through the numbers reflect the huge lobbying pressure presented by Special Interests, both inside and outside the Government. The distribution process begins, with each member of Congress insistent upon on a fair share of the Pork Barrel; aforesaid used to purchase support in their districts. All work with the confidence the Pork Barrel can be funded from reduction of the Budget Proposals; these proposals somehow providing legitimacy to the level of Federal Expenditure. Congress feels justified as they shave Twenty percent off the Budget Proposals on average, to fund Pork Barrel; proclaiming great service to their Constituents.

Federal Departments, Agencies, and Committees howl, as is properly political for the Public as their Budget Proposals have been cut; and whose actual Budget for the Year stands approximately Twenty percent higher than the actual Wish List. The Funds start to drain through the Department, each level drawing off their own discretionary funds (about Ten percent higher than actual expenses), until the lowest level is reached. They receive the level they gained the previous year, with no more than a Five percent gain; some Sixty percent of their initial Wish List. This level dealing with the actual Public, generally manages to subsist on this funding; but if they cannot, they receive funds from intermediate levels upon defined need. All departments enjoying about a Twenty percent over-funding, with Everyone happy.

Trouble arises in the Third Quarter of the Fiscal Year. Civil Service dogma contains the adage 'All budgeted funds must be spent, else Congress may drastically reduce the next Budget Proposal'. Exploratory and Training trips are increased for all Employment levels, which can absorb maybe Twenty percent of the excess funds. Paid Vacations with paid accommodations for Employees are planned, which can absorb another Thirty percent of the excess. The final resort is initiated, and new Employees are hired; to help with the work level, only One-quarter of Private sector equivalent duties. Sharing excess funds with Public Citizens may never be considered; for such would exceed departmental empowerment by Congress. Benefit must go to Civil Servants, not American Taxpayers or Welfare indigent.

The Budgetary process starts once more, and Everyone again forms their Wish List. Civil Service dogma also states every Budget Proposal must exceed that of the previous Year. This stands as absolute, even if the department lost half of it's Welfare Recipients; or in the case of the Military, lost the Weapon system through acceptance or rejection for the next stage. Only complete shutdown of the specific departmental area allows for a reduced Budget Proposal. This shutdown process is functionally impossible in Civilian agency; accomplishable in the Military, only by complete transfer of all personnel. The Wish Lists grow at about Five percent per year, while actual Congressional dispensation grows about Two percent per year.

Overcoming Civil Service dogma of such entrenched magnitude will require resolution by Congress and President. A interesting avenue may be to set up a Control system at the Treasury. Congress could mandate the Treasury to refuse release Budgeted funds to any department, except by Quarter-Year Periods. Intrinsic to this action would be a demand on all departments of Government to set up Two-Week expenditure pattern Budgets every Fiscal Year. The Treasury would be mandated not to release the next Quarter-Year allotment, until the department had less funds than a Two-Week allotment. Congress could examine these Two-Week expenditure pattern budgets, searching for excess funding; reducing this budget as desired, with Treasury mandate to restrict funding to this budget.

The structure of Fiscal Budgeting would be deeply altered by this budgeting pattern. The publication of this bi-weekly expenditures budget allows for close examination by Congress and Treasury. Wastage can be identified by Congress, or Congressional staff. Curative action effected solely by notification to the Treasury. Redress by Federal department would be limited to proof expenditure patterns were actually higher; then only on elements acceptable to Congress. Many of the elements of Private enterprise supervision will be introduced, still with allowance for the special nature of Government operation. This factor alone could reverse the growth of Civil Service employment, with attrition of retirement from Civil Service. Total estimate of potential per year savings to American Taxpayers could reach $35-40 Billion.

A real outcome of the above procedure may be a betterment of Public benefit per dollar spent. Dollars not spent on Civil Service cadres will undoubtedly be transferred to Program fulfillment in Federal budgeting. This means the needs of American citizens for which the Programs were designed, will be increasingly funded. Economic strata dictate declines in Government expenditures lead to failures of economic performance. Congress and President will be inclined to continue these expenditures for Economic success; bringing increased funding for the needs of private Citizens. This transfer of funds to the private Citizens concerned may lead to an increase in the Standard of Living up to Fifteen percent.

A final note for this Chapter must contain the call for the creation of a new Federal Agency; called the Weapons Development and Special Projects Agency. This Agency would consist solely of Investigative Auditors, or the Agency described as the Government's internal Accounting Firm. Their sole function will be to examine all Weapons systems under development, or Special Projects assigned by Congress; and to do so in a proscribed manner. Comparison of Weapons development with current in-use weapons system; not only in terms of Cost in development and per-unit Cost, but also in comparative effectiveness. Another element to be considered will be degree of similarity. A developing Weapon system which must duplicate current in-use weaponry to attain the level of proficiency demanded, must be reported to Congress. The whole purpose of this Agency will be placement of the developing Weapons systems in the prospective of current armament. Most may suggest this would be repetitious bureaucratic waste; the Author replies if this Agency were involved in all aspects of Research and Development, maybe half of the current Weapon system under development would be canceled, because of lack of viability. This would mean a savings of 15-30 Billion dollars per year.

5
The Federal Personal Information Agency

Every Businessman and Citizen complains about the level of paper-work demanded by the bureaucratic structure under which We all live. Successive efforts have been made to reduce the number of forms American Citizens must fill out, and the additional number which Civil Servants are required to fill out for each Case. These efforts reached doom, by trying to work with the current system. Asking Civil Servants what Forms are absolutely mandatory, constitute an act of folly; they will always come up with a greater number, than are currently present. Bureaucrats can only think along bureaucratic lines. Another style solution must be derived.

The Author suggests the creation of a Federal Personal Information Agency. The establishment of another bureaucracy will accomplish nothing, unless specific Congress-mandated ground rules apply. These ground rules must specifically prohibit bureaucratic procedures from entering into the matrix. Astute examination must be utilized, to close loopholes which Bureaucrats will naturally exploit. The Author here gives his best attempt.

The Federal Personal Information Agency will be empowered by Congress. It's enabling Act precludes any other Department, Agency, or Agent of the Federal Government from the retention of records on any Individual or Business on American soil. All Information will be kept in electronic form alone; the proposed Agency to backup all files on Computers not connected to any phone lines, with addition disk copies held in protected storage. Level of Access to information stored will be set from One to Ten. The bottom level will be only Name, address and contact information, Social Security number, and Work contact. IRS will have access to Level Eight; Law Enforcement Agencies and Agents Level Nine, and National Security and Intelligence Agency will be given Level Ten—total access. All Government employees must input all information in electronically from their Work location; they are to attain this information from Interview and Phone Interview, all Forms are forbidden with no information requests allowed in written form to Public Citizens. All information on Citizens will be kept until it can be verified or disproved from three sources. An intelligent Congress would dictate the rules apply to State and Local Government Agencies, as well as Federal departments.

Examination of the Proposal brings better understanding. The establishment of one sole Agency to store Personal Information on Individuals and Businesses provides better security of said information from misappropriation. Miles of Paper will be saved from destruction every year, with a Budget saving of almost $11 Billion per year. Access to the information can be tightly controlled, with unitary security measures; so all departments will express greater efficiency, dealing only with such information they are allowed. The reduction of necessary Man-hours devoted to the reading of superfluous data will be curtailed, as will the filling out of Forms; to an expected saving of $4 Billion per year. The period of processing will be reduced, providing a potential gain to applicant Citizen of perhaps $20 Billion per year. Speed of Government function will overall increase.

Elimination of on-site Paper records will cut potential necessary Federal office space by a possible One-half; saving a possible $30 Billion per year. Elimination of personal receipts to Applicants provide another $6 Billion per year in unnecessary Printing costs; accomplishable with a standard Private Citizen access code consisting of 'www.Gov.SS.personalsocialsecuritynumber' where all Government personal approvals as listed. This process will be aided by Public access Reception desks being equipped with Computer units with double screens and keyboards, like back-to-back PCs; enabled for Government employees to lead Private Citizens to every informational site to be filled out, or information found. Privacy will be insured by the Public side Screen being shut down, unless the proper Social Security number has been logged in. This will eliminate half of all Personal records Private citizens are forced to keep, and all necessary information can be checked, by both Government employee and private citizen.

Greater security could be attained, if the Federal Government would enter the Twentieth Century now We are in the Third Millennium; and issue Charge-card style Identification cards. Access to Personal information could then be limited only to Government authorized Computer stations; where One had to insert the Card, then type in the proper Date of Birth in numerals as a security code. This may seem as a very simplistic security measure; but would be Ninety-five percent effective. Limitation to the level of access except with clearance provided by Government employee at allowed Government office, finishes the primary need for Security. Individual Citizen's personal desire for general receipts and acknowledgments can be derived at Government-authorized stations situated at Libraries, Government offices, and Banks.

The Congress of the United States must enter into discussion of the Issue of Privacy. Neither Court or Congress has ever directly addressed the overall Issue. Congress must define what levels of Privacy violation Government agencies are allowed to collect; then define precisely who and what entities of Government will have what level of access to the collected information. This definition must withstand the onslaught of the Courts. The Issue becomes ever more vital, now in the Age of the War on Terrorism. Law enforcement agencies increasingly invade areas previously out-of-bounds, with the tacit assent of the Courts; who refuse to rule on the transgressions, in the interest of National Security.

The real consensus will devolve into acceptance of the gathering of all information, simply because Government Agents and Agencies remain more terrorized by the new Terrorism than common citizens. The new Terrorists target Government offices, or those facilities which those Government Agents use with great frequency. Protection from Personal and Family threat has entered the equation for Government personnel, even for Judicial figures. Otherwise reasonable limitations of access to Privacy elements, will not be rigidly enforced.

There can be no sensible expectation of a good limitation to the invasion of Privacy. The context of the Privacy Issue must be re-examined. The acquirement of Personal information will not be effectively restrained, so Congress must limit the use of this information. Legislation must be passed restricting this information to the Authorities, where such knowledge is automatically mandatory. Criminal Penalties must be assigned to misuse of this information, by type of offense engendered. Individual Civil Action must be sanctioned by law, for defamation of Character through release of Personal information; set up for payment of real damages, and specified punitive damages. The Government employee must be constrained to treat this Personal information with due respect.

A most important element operating in the Court system is the preclusion of information of prior offense, to those who must make judgmental decisions. We cannot abide this ridiculous facade in attempts to provide the Accused with a second chance. The level of deliverable violence and destruction capable even for the non-technologically proficient, forestalls such short-sighted fictions. Congress must insure legislation allowing law enforcement agents, Judges, Juries, and Journalists full access to the Accused's Arrest and Conviction records. All of the above need to know the level of violence to which the Accused can be capable. This legislation should also entail specific punishments, for the violations of the rights of an Individual; but prohibit the release of known guilty parties, specifically because their civil liberties have been violated. This Age of Pocket-sized Mass Destruction precludes retention of antiqued formulations of operation.

Legislation establishing the proposed Federal Personal Information Agency should break new ground. Repetitive requests for Information should be specifically forbidden. Options could be preclusion from inputting information, except through certain Agencies. The IRS, law enforcement agencies, and the Social Security administrators could be the only designates allowed to input Personal addresses, telephone numbers, levels of income, sources of income, legal arrests and convictions, physical identification features, physical disabilities or deformities, and personal relationships. Medical Agencies and Social Security administrators named designates to enter medical information on the Individual. Taxing agencies alone allowed to list Capital assets and Property of the Individual. Military authorities alone allowed to list the military service records of an Individual. Educational agencies alone empowered to collect and distribute educational records of the Individual. This compartmentalization of Access input with proper setting of Access levels, will not only bring greater Privacy for the Individual; it will also eliminate vast duplication of effort by Government employees. These Civil Servants will restrict themselves to the necessary information for their jobs; bringing much discrimination to an end, and cutting a huge number of labor hours from the Government work schedule.

One valid rationale for the new Agency would be the creation of an American Doomsday Book. There still remains no unified Graphic of American territory; in terms of Ownership, use of the property, and population placement. The accurate definition of every square foot of property in terms of title to it, lies only at the distributed County level of taxing agencies. Federal and States agencies only use their overall records. Most County Records have never had an update, since the initial recording of property, somewhere in the Nineteenth Century. All of which is recorded remains transferences of title, and the tax billing of listed Ownership. Title searches are currently conducted only on

Computer; without resort to moldy records in dusty Courthouse basements. No One makes a grid search of Maps, to check if the Tax Lists are accurate. Many Counties and Parishes own Property which was condemned for Tax Default, without later purchase at Auction. The files were simply stored and forgotten. The state of records at the Dept. of the Interior stand in worse shape. Identification of Property alone, with it's placement on Computer at a national agency; allows for collation of data.

Some believe, including this Author, approximately One percent of total land in this Country lacks Tenant owner; said fact known only to paper County Records never checked. The major manner this derived, was through death of Tenant owner; without notification of County Records. The lack of heirs, or lack of interest in the Property by those heirs; brought Tax default not properly recorded. This default may have occurred prior to the introduction of the Computer; or applied through sloppy reportage and documentation. The general rule of Sheriff's Auctions state Property not purchased through Three Auctions; will not be offered at Auction again. County Records' has no interest, after the Sale Request is sent to the Sheriff. The Sheriff's buries the Sales Request in his own files, if there is not immediate Sale of the Property. The County Assessors check by Computer on the Property every year, to find a Sales Request has been sent to the Sheriff; interest drops in the matter at that point.

Everyone knows of old Houses in their Community, where no One has lived for years; this is because a Sales Request resides in a Sheriff's Department file, in over Seventy percent of the cases. Likewise the abandoned Business sites, with often no Person stepping on site in decades. Rural communities even have abandoned farmsteads, even with the high price of farmland; simply because initial Auctions brought no Purchasers. Subsequent Auctions have not been held. There are entire streets in Cities, both residential and Business districts; where Sheriff's Auction produce no Purchasers, because the entire area has been abandoned, and where Purchasers would pay much higher prices only blocks away; because of habitation or traffic.

A simple central authority could require all County Agents, including Sheriffs, to forward all Property information; all such information checked by Computer, to find gaps in the Graphics. Investigators next sent to location to research the gaps; researching Records and with on-site inspection. The Military could find all it's forgotten Property, the Federal Government could outline a compiled list of it's Property assets, and State and County officials could be notified of valuable Property assets for potential Sale or development.

An important Employment program to train Welfare Recipients for gainful work, could be integrated into this Agency. Most Unemployed and Welfare Recipients today know how to operate Computers. Local area Unemployed could be hired at Minimum Wages for the transference of non-transferred County Records to Computer. Such costs would be minimal; simply the cost of the Computer equipment and Wages, which could subtract from welfare payments made. This transference could have great historical value, let local authorities eliminate physical file space, and locate lost essential information.

The intrinsic value of a centralized Information Agency vastly exceeds both it's cost, and it's Security threat. Effective implementation would eliminate unnecessary labor hours from the Federal work schedule, identify Federal properties and their use, eliminate vast irritation for Private Citizens overburdened by the informational demands of their Government, and reduce total Federal Employment. Most of the cost of such a Federal Information Agency may be recouped from State and Local Governments; simply because the efficiency of the system would lead to their rental of services from the Information agency. An effective program leads this Author to envision a Federal, State, and Local employment rate near half of Today's rate. The gathered material would have great Historical and Educational potential as well; allowing for statistical analysis of trends.

Economics would benefit incredibly from such a centralized wealth of Information. Economists would derive ability to track daily Treasury dispersals; categorizing them by Sector, and funding Power. They could track daily Consumer Credit balances. Tracking of Resource flow would become easy. Transport could be accounted daily, with Transport numbers accurately recounted; all to find shortage areas and congestions. Daily Production figures would be at hand, and evaluation speeded to half the time. Economic prediction becomes forecasting, like the weather; which is now a successful Science.

6
Function of Government

The American Public possesses a schizophrenic attitude towards Government, and has since the Republican administration and Congress of 1863. The Republican Party in the Nineteenth Century was the Party of Big Government, while the Democratic Party served as the bulwark of small, local, decentralized Government. The Republicans held the mantle of the Big Government Party, until the advent of World War I. The Republicans during this Sixty Year period managed to build the Railway system by land grants to Railroads, establish the State University and College system, establish a National Park system, set Child Labor laws, organize the Food and Drug Administration, and originate the Federal Reserve System. The Democratic Party during this same Period organized the City Political machines, which established a wide base of power, based upon the welfare triage of the Poor of the inner-Cities. The decade of the 1920s were dedicated to building Cities and the national Roadway system, neither Party concerned with Government much; as long as it did not interfere to any great degree, with the plans of either Party. Then came the Great Depression.

This cataclysmic Event tore deep divisions in the American political fabric. The Republican Party was totally discredited, long at the helm of American Government. Calvin Coolidge's 'The Business of America is Business' sounded hollow, with half of the production capacity of the Country shut down. Huge numbers of long-standing Supporters of the Republican Party were themselves standing in the lines at the Soup

Kitchens. Herbert Hoover could not present potential solutions to the Crisis; without direct conflict with the wealthy backbone of the Party. This Man who had fed Millions of Europe through disastrous circumstances; becomes known as the 'Do-Nothing' President, who would let the American People starve.

The Democratic Party, itself, faced horrid threat; the welfare triage of inner-City Poor served as their base of Power, yet, the numbers of Poor had risen beyond the triage capacities of the Democratic Party. The Democratic Party had to abandon their decentralized concept of Government; in order to gain Government assumption of the welfare triage of the Poor. The Great Depression left the Republican Party with the image of indifference to American livelihood; and propelled the Democratic Party into the role of advocate of Big Brother Government.

The metamorphism for both Parties brought an incredible growth for Government, especially at the national level. The Republicans retained their use of Government welfare for Business; while the Democratic Party gave up their welfare triage of the Poor, to gain Votes by promulgation of Welfare programs. Supply-Siders face off against Welfare Activists today; One wanting funding for Business, the other funding for People. Neither want a reduction of Spending; Both want the supporters of the other Party to pay for the funding of the Expenditure flow.

Both Parties, Today, are addicted to the Pork Barrel; no One wanting a true measurable decrease in Government. Democrats want huge expenditure on People programs, to gain the support of American families. Republicans want lucrative Contracts from Government construction; building Profits for their Supporters in the Business world. Democrats are turning increasingly to Republican ways, to get Business support. Republicans scream about support for Social Security and Medicare, to attain the support of the Middle Class; who most benefit from such programs. The advent of the Clinton administration brought a Republican Pork Barrel Artist, with a Welfare agenda. The Bush administration has brought the first Two Trillion Dollar Budget.

The entire discussion of the National Debt amplifies the impact of operating experience on current American Politicians. The first real expansion of the Debt came with World War II. The entire theme at the time was winning the World for Democracy. A War between regional Powers demonized for great effort, with huge charges laid on the American people with the smell of religious fervor. Confrontation with the Soviet Union and the Cold War became the replacement excuse for huge expenditure. Promotion of the Economy followed with the Kennedy administration, then the War on Poverty of Johnson, and blended in the 1970s into Government as Employer of Last Resort. Ronald Reagan brought Us the Evil Empire as external Villain, and Government welfare as Evil of the Interior. Clinton could feel the pain of the Poor, but the explosion of American Production from proper tax rates; reversed the accumulation of Debt for the first time since Roosevelt took office in 1932, except for One year in the 1950s. There is hardly a Politician left, who was not born in the Age of Deficit Spending.

Greenspan, the head of the Federal Reserve, comments too rapid a reduction of the National Debt would eliminate a major tool of Monetarist Economists; the purchase or sale of Treasury Securities by the Federal Reserve to regulate the Money Supply. This Author does not claim to have read the Library of Monetarist literature, finding the entire field boring and uneventful; yet, finds the idea unworthy of distinguished Economists. The purchase of Securities to expand the Money Supply pursues a relatively ineffective course; the expansion of the Money Supply depending upon the speed of the Economy (i.e., the rapidity of Production and Purchase rates). Liquidity will not speed these rates, and releases of significant amounts of Cash into the Economy; can be proven only to spur Inflation, by the venue of hard statistical data. The Federal Reserve need not limit itself only to the purchase of Federal Securities, if statistical data is ever delivered to prove the thesis such purchases can spur Economic performance; Congress could easily empower the Federal Reserve to purchase State and Local Bond issuances, even if It wanted to limit purchase of securities from the Private Sector.

There is further argument the National Debt somehow softens the American Dollar in the International markets, so it will be cheaper for Foreigners to purchase American Goods. The strength of the American Dollar stands upon an equation: the total quantity of Goods and Services produced by the American Economy, divided by the total number of Dollars paid for them. Many will think the Author has reversed the equation, but he has not; the strength of the Dollar is estimated as a percentage ratio. This ratio is also the manner in which to figure proper Inflation rates. The question arises on the correct manner of defining the quantity of Goods and Services produced. This is a difficult equation hotly debated, whenever brought up; almost never! This Author likes the total number of recorded Labor hours times the total tons of Resources utilized, divided by the total amount of Capital Equipment in tonnage. The Author admittedly grants he has never used this equation, because of the inability to aggregate the data; luckily, he is only an Economic Theorist. This trip to the Ozone layer was presented only to point out; the level of Government debt has nothing to do with the strength of the Dollar.

What is the addiction of American Politicians to the promulgation of Debt, to the degree the Bush administration pushes policies destined to return to Deficit spending? The answer must be the American political process, Itself, fueled this addiction. Business and Businessmen, or the people made wealthy by them, provide almost Eighty percent of Political contributions. No Politician would think to challenge the Business interests among his Constituents. The Reader may ask why this could be important. They may believe Business interests are in favor of rational expenditure patterns for Government.

Two reasons exist why Business dislike Government surpluses. The first says there is an incredible amount of Investment capital wrapped up in the National Debt. The Holders of the Debt are Investors; paying off the National Debt, would mean a release of a great amount of Investment capital, the Holders not known for enlarging their Consumption patterns. This payment of the National Debt would mean a vast increase of competition in the Private Sector; whose profit rates are currently enjoyed by Business interests. These Profits ratios would fall substantially with the introduction of such levels of Investment capital entering the Private Sector.

The second reason for Deficit spending returns to the Profit ratios of Business interest once more. Business interests benefit directly by deficit spending by Government. It does not matter whether they are supplying Products for the magnified Consumption patterns of the Poor, or enjoying lucrative Government contracts; deficit spending reflect as higher Profits for business interests, largesse conservatively estimated at Twelve percent of the Total. The amounts available can easily pay for the entire Labor Costs throughout their entire Production; simply dependent upon the Profits derived. Many would doubt this proposition; it is sufficient to state General Motors can pay it's entire Labor Costs bill, through lease and sale of vehicles to the three levels of Government it serves. It is in the interest of General Motors to insure there are sufficient Government employees to drive those vehicles. Canned foods sell more of their total volume to subsidized Poor, than they do Wage-Earners. American Business interests possess a total Sales market approximately 1.3 times the size otherwise allowed, if Government welfare payments did not foot the bill. They would fight reduction of those Welfare payments; until and unless, an alternate form of payment was already in place.

Politicians quickly learn Business interests want no interruptions in their Profits. Rhetoric appeals to Middle Class values of self-reliance notwithstanding; political contributions come from high Government expenditure. Business interests want a high volume of Sales, even if the Government has to pay for those Sales. Reductions of Government expenditure is political suicide, even when the Economy is expanding with welfare rolls reducing; Business simply perceives the reduction as a curtailment of Profits. Business has not surrendered the concept of Government as the Employer of Last Resort.

Government has never left any area of Society it has ever entered, not matter for whatever reason entered; and never will, because of embedded interests whose only concern lies in perpetuated expenditures. These expenditures, though, are quickly approaching levels unacceptable to either Economist or Taxpayer. Social Security assures the welfare roles will increase for years, what with the Baby Boomers reaching retirement age. Social Security payments can easily triple, while the Labor supporting those payments; will decrease in number, with these retirements. Solutions must be found.

The first element which must be attacked, can only be the practice of retirement. It must be noted earlier call was for a unitary monthly Social Security payment of sufficient size to pay living costs for Beneficiaries. This payment should be limited to just meeting those living needs. The reason is provision of pressure on the Elderly to work, where they are able. This helps to contain severe reduction of the Labor force. This incentive to work can be enhanced by removal of all restrictions on the levels of Income Retirees can earn. The best way to accomplish this is the retention of taxation of Social Security benefits, when the Beneficiaries' income is too high; but to give them a 100% deduction from their Income tax of all Income from a Job, working for a business or organization not their own. Retirees would be enticed to report all such Income, instead of hiding it as done Today; and search for lucrative positions, even when they have great amounts of Income from other sources. Retirees must understand Government wants their efforts, as long as those efforts can be provided.

The second element must be the integration of welfare programs. States currently operate Unemployment services. They should continue to provide the basic Job Search procedure. The Government should pass legislation which withdraws Unemployment benefits from the States; putting Social Security in charge of such payments. The

Program for this Action must be very precise. Payments should start within Ten Days of notification. Payments are to be made monthly, and not exceed the unitary monthly Social Security benefit; set up as the minimum necessary to pay basic living needs. The State where the Unemployed is resident, will be immediately notified; and will verify the Unemployed is actually unemployed. The resident State of the Unemployed will have to pay One-third of the monthly standard benefit, the former Employer will have to pay One-third of the monthly standard benefit, and the Social Security Fund will pay One-third.

This method of payment assures the resident State holding the Unemployed will have to pay the amount corresponding to regular payments of the Individual into the Fund. The former Employer will be bound for effective Severance pay; limited to a Six month period considered a normal Unemployment period, with the Social Security Fund assuming the additional One-third after that Period. The Individual will also be made responsible for his Unemployment as well. His Social Security withholding tax will be Ten percent higher, when he returns to Work, until the total payments made by Social Security is repaid figured in numbers of Weeks of enhanced tax. All other forms of assistance to this Individual will be disallowed; except for a Ten percent increase in monthly benefit per Unemployed's Dependent without exterior income.

The whole Unemployment payment schedule becomes rationalized, with the responsibility replaced on the Individual to find work. The welfare payments serve to restrict Inflation, holding down Rents and Product price increases; due to the refusal to extend other benefits. The viability of the Individual to regain viable Employment is maintained, while maintaining the security of the Social Security Fund. The general Federal Government funds can be easily used to supplement the Social Security Fund, under conditions of extended widespread Unemployment. The Author suggests a floor be implicit in Law, stating Social Security revenues must exceed Social Security expenditures; so that the level of the current Fund can be maintained, along with any growth.

General Government funds must make up the Shortfall. The tiered level of payment should assure these transfers will never be significant, to the degree Government budgeting is distorted.

The Author previously (PLANS FOR THE FUTURE, Xlibris 2000) asserted the Educational system should be modified. The basic alteration would be the manner of payment; shifted off local Communities per se, and burden placed on those most benefitted by educational opportunity: Employers and Employees. The base tax consists of a per-hour tax placed on hours worked. Properly managed, such a system would be no greater charge against any Employer or Employee; with potential rebates for Employers unduly affected. The real Economic rationale for this change, comes in the devotion of Property taxes to fulfillment of local Community needs—police, fire, ambulance service, and Community services. Such devotion of Property taxes would reduce the need for Federal and State assistance for these Communities; to less than Ten percent of current needs. The modified tax would also force Employers to budget a real training cost into their Production schedules, instead of the current system; which evades payment for the basic necessities training, due to misplacement of burden.

Another element cited in the above listed Work, consists in the thought Local School Boards need be tasked with the total care of the children in the Community. Local School Boards are elected by the Community, are intensely supervised by Parents in the area, and have the in-place facilities to expand on their current role. The expansion of this role would consist of both day-care and potential night-care, provision of medical and dental care for all students, provision of Three meals per day, and clothing where necessary. Local School Boards would be empowered supervision of the children, with the power to remove the child from the Parental home upon sign of abuse or neglect. They must hire all appropriate personnel, and insure proper supervision of such personnel.

School Board responsibility for these children would extend from birth until age Eighteen for the children. This Plan envisions a great expansion of responsibilities for School Boards. The cost will probably quadruple the current budgets. The above-mentioned Work-hour Tax would fund the greatest majority of the extended budgets. Parents would be charged a weekly Meal cost for each of their children; application made to State welfare or Federal assistance, if the expense proves too costly. They would also be charged on a pro-rated, per-child basis for all medical and dental care; paid on a Monthly basis, also subject of assistance. A uniform dress code would allow for a Monthly set Clothing Allowance to be charged to the Parents. The beauty of the Plan consists of the assurance to the Parents, closely supervised by self-same Parents; their children will be taken care of, properly fed, given medical and dental care at cheaper rates, all with maximum supervision The Collective payment will provide better care, greater trained supervision, and better health care; than does the current system of sporadic subsistence.

The transfer of Care responsibilities to the Educational system allows for the elimination of Aid to Dependent Children. Single Mothers will be left with no excuse for receipt of welfare assistance; day and night care will be available for their children on a 24/7 basis, from the date of their child's birth. Provision will undoubtedly be made for Single Mothers to utilize dormitory housing, until the child is born, along with some period of recovery. They will be expected to seek employment for themselves, shortly after birth; with responsibility for their own support. School Boards will be empowered to fill out support papers for State or Federal Child assistance themselves, and only payments to School Boards will be made; Parents cannot benefit from necessary Child assistance, and School Boards will possess the power of garnishment of Parental wages to collect Child support payments. The proposed system provides greater care, at less cost to both Parents and Government.

Conservatives will undoubted accuse this Plan as a huge increase in Federal power. They would be wrong! Local elected officials would administrate the program; hiring qualified personnel, receiving all dispensed funds, setting the quality of care within boundaries of Federal Health supervision, establishing the educational and recreational standards for the children, and punishing delinquent Parents. Parental abuse or negligence will be decriminalized, unless the child has been injured; School Boards simply removing custody for the Child from the Parent, with only supervised contact with the Child. The most effective, and cheapest Child care will be the norm, removing a heavy burden from working Parents. Much of the heavy rigor of Parentage will be removed; while the joys and access to the Child will be maximized.

Discussion of the Budget burden for such a Plan must be advanced. Many would claim the extension would cost a fortune; this Author estimates the Plan would cost less than the current Military budget of the Federal Government, which the Bush administration intends to increase. The Work-hour Tax can be estimated to increase the real Tax burden of Business in this Country, by about Three percent; or a sum raising their current real tax payments by about Fourteen percent. The removal of School support from the Property Tax burden, will not likely reduce the Property tax rate; it will simply eliminate the need of Federal Assistance programs, to pay State and Local Governments for extreme area expenses. Astute administration of the program at the Federal level could even save the Federal Budget somewhere around Fifty Billion dollars per year, over current expenditures; while raising the quality of Child Care.

Discussion of Government welfare to Business always aroused the ire of Conservatives. They dismiss Government contracts as normal Business contracts, and deny any interdiction to their operation. They ignore Federal Government contracts are the only Contracts in the World which habitually pay all Research and Development costs, often pay all Capital equipment costs, have intrinsic full Profits guarantees, and automatic renewal guarantees. These Contracts traditionally possess no financial liabilities for failure to meet the Schedules stipulated, Cost overruns, or substandard labor and quality. They generally stipulate payment with guaranteed Profitability, even if the Product or Service is rejected. The Contracts often even guarantee a Balloon Severance payment possibly up to the full value of the Contract, if Congress denies successive funding. The Author does not believe these Contracts are normal Business contracts.

Several alteration to Federal Contract Law could be enacted by Congress. Failure to meet Schedule dates in the Contract could be mandated to reduce guaranteed Profitability by Fifteen percent. Research and Development Costs over the stipulated numbers of the Contract; will only be paid at a rate of Ninety Percent of the amount in excess. All automatic renewal provisions will be removed from Government Contracts; all renewal will be reviewed for efficiency. Substandard Labor or Quality issues will be fined by reduction of the Contract payment for the total of Labor hours involved. All Profitability provisions for the Contract will be automatically removed, paying only for the actual Cost; if the Product or Service is rejected. Refusal of Congressional funding will be stated to mean just that; no Severance payments will be allowed, unless actual unpaid Research or Production has already been conducted at the time of Funding refusal. Most will claim this complicates the Federal Contracting process, removing incentive for Business to enter into such Contracts. The Author asserts the level of Profits in Government Contracting remains abnormally high, and willing Business elements will be found. He goes on to assert such alteration will save American Taxpayers a Trillion Dollars, over the next Twenty years.

The Costs associated with the Judicial system in the United States go beyond the bounds of human reason. Legal fees exceed the percentage total Labor figures of any Country in the World; reimbursement for legal services in this Country remain almost double those of the next Contender. The above can be explained as it costing almost Three times as much to put a Criminal in Prison in the United States, as anywhere else in the World. Lawyers draw almost twice the percentage of Total Wages paid, as in any other Country. The percentages only worsen when researched in terms of per Ten Thousand Worker units. This has profound impact on the Cost of the Courts.

The Public Defender system remains a source of widespread abuse. Public Defenders file almost three times as many legal documents, than do their opposite numbers in other Countries; when defending for the same type of Crime. Death Sentence Cases generally have a duration of around Twenty-two years, and legal fees generally cost Four times as much; as keeping the Convicted in Prison, for his entire life. Legal petitions of lawyers for Convicts already in Prison has risen by 12,000%, in the last Twenty years; almost all paid for by American Taxpayers. All of the above legal paperwork leads to an Eighty percent Conviction rate, with only a Two percent reversal rate. The only significant element in all this effort, stands at lawyers being paid more than $30 per hour for this work; legally, almost all paid by Taxpayers.

This largesse affects the States far more than the Federal level; yet, a more rationalized Judicial system would cut in half the appeals made to the Federal Courts; an estimate without hard numbers, suggests up to Three Billion dollars in Savings. Other aspects of the cost of the Legal System trouble even more. No numbers exist anywhere, outlining the number of lawyers employed by the Federal Government, in one capacity or another. This Author horridly wonders if this number does not exceed the regular Military complement of this Nation. It is enough to establish their yearly remuneration stands at approximately Four times that of an NCO. It is also known lawyers employed by the Federal Government exceed in number, all serving Military officers. Suffice it to stipulate these Federally-employed lawyers make up a huge percentage of total graduates of this Nation's Law Schools. The rate of Pay is inevitably better than $30 per hour.

The above paragraph was given to highlight the potential advantage in establishing a different context for legal conduct by the Federal Government. The multiplicity of Forms issued by the Federal Government, probably stands as the most productive process in the Government. Why can't they do the same for legal affairs? This Author proposes the creation of a Legal Contract Agency. The new bureau-cracy would be empowered to write standardized legal contracts, checked by the Federal Courts for legality; whose rulings would give the standardized forms the force of Law. These Contracts would then be mandated for use in all contractual agreements made by the Federal Government. These standardized Contracts are to be so diverse and detailed, only Names and numbers need be entered. Ordinary Man-agement levels of Civil Service, if empowered to do so; could handle Contract negotiations themselves, without the advent or advise of employed lawyers. Technical negotiations of great finesse could be handled by Employees of the Legal Contract Agency itself.

The number of lawyers employed by the Legal Contract Agency should be mandated by Law not to exceed 2,000 in number, with a total number of Employees set at 5,000. The Agency would be legally mandated to provide all Contracts for the Federal Government, with only negotiation with Agency lawyers allowed for Contract derivations. The Author seriously doubts the number of employed lawyers could even be cut in half; but still expects over an $8 Billion saving from the Federal Budget.

The next proposal must be a Government Retirement Agency. Civil Service and Military Retirement policies are so diverse, and spread so much largesse; action should be taken to counteract excess charges. Congress should create the above Agency, simply to cut Costs in this process. The Empowerment should contain several provisions. The first must be the Agency will handle all pensions and disabilities for the Federal Government, without even Congress being exempt. The sec-ond must be all Pensions must be based as multiples of the standard, or Average, monthly benefits granted by Social Security to retirees. The third stipulation must be only Four classifications of Pensions will be entertained: Ordinary Labor, Middle Management and Specialist, Upper Management, and Program Directors and Elected Officials. The fourth provision must be a minimum of Twelve Years necessary to draw Pension benefits, even for Elected officials; the only exemption being the President of the United States. The benefits would be estimated upon Twenty years of Service, percentage alterations for alternate terms of Service, above or below Twenty years Service. The fifth must be all benefits must be standard for each level. Most would say such an Agency would not make a difference, though retired Congressmen would have to defend a retirement benefit Twenty-eight times the standard, or Averaged, monthly Social Security benefit. Such a Conversion could save American Taxpayers more than $30 Billion per year.

The last recommendation to be registered is the declaration that the Civil Service Workweek should be reduced to 32 hours. The Author has long been an advocate of the 32 hour Workweek for the Private Sector. The shorter Workweek would bring an appreciable increase in the productivity, create more extensive trained labor reserves, layoffs would reduce to Twenty percent of the current rate, better scheduling of Work schedules could be effected, and lower training costs could be expected than is the increased schedules after each layoff. The Author asserts payment of Overtime over 32 hours, is much cheaper than the above losses. He here doubts any of the above gains, when contemplating a reduction of the Civil Service Workweek. Civil Servants remain unnoted for increasing Output under any conditions. The advantages of a shorter Civil Service Workweek stand as better scheduling efforts, lower immediate Wages paid out, lower benefits paid out, greater incentive to limit Careers to Twenty years, easier transfers to more productive areas, and actual reduction of Travel, excess use of Medical days, and lower per Employee labor costs.

Civil Servants find less excuse to be away from their Workplace, under conditions of a 3-day Weekend. This has been proven by a number of States, who use the 32-hour Workweek during the summer, for their Academic institutions. Productivity was actually shown to have gone up, as the offices were open only Four days. Federal offices would have Employees in Two shifts: those who work Monday through Thursday, and those who work Tuesday through Friday. The offices would be fully staffed through the power-days of the Week. Actual labor expense costs would go down, with less use of Paper, Energy, and Computer wear. Public crowding of access areas could actually decrease, as actual speed of Case load increases. Employees would be under pressure to finish current Cases, before the end of the Workweek.

Actual labor costs for the Federal Government would diminish dramatically. Only Four-fifths of the Labor hours would be clocked. The number of Medical leave days should decrease to Sixty percent of the Current rate. Personal time could be reduced by an actual Week of payment, when there is a death in the family. Legislation could be used to limit Vacation time to Four Weeks, a great saving as 37% of the Civil Service get more than Four Weeks; even if this legislation is not enacted, the reduced Workweek would save almost a Week's payment per Employee vacation. The total saving from the shortened Workweek cannot be quantatively set, though it is estimated to exceed $17 Billion per year.

All the measures proposed in this Chapter are relatively easy to implement, were it not for the extreme political opposition to such changes. This political opposition carries a real misplacement; the standard of living of Civil Servants can be actually expected to increase under a new program. There will be real opportunity to seek Part-time employment, utilizing their skills attained under Federal training programs. Incentives will be present to take those skills fully to the Private Sector sooner than the average Twenty-four years at Present, because of the higher Pay rates available after fulfilling the minimum full Pension enablement. The extra day off allow for search of better Employment opportunities, reducing Federal Pension costs; if the provision of a minimum of Twelve years for Pension vestment is passed. The increased Federal training costs would be easily offset, by the lower Pension benefits paid. Federal Disabilities payments can be expected to reduce faster than the Work reduction, somewhere around 28 percent of the Current level; due to the average reduced Civil Service Career length, and the reduction of the total repetitive work conducted. Total

Civil Service labor medical costs would be expected to only reduce by 16%, due to addition of Civil Service Retiree medical programs.

More efficient Government Contracting would allow for secure scheduling of Production capacities; with switch to private production concurrently run, for double use of Productive capacity. Research and Development would become more highly proficient, as avenues were discontinued more quickly. R&D assets could be turned to alternative programs, both Public and Private. Reduced Government expenditures allow investment in Standard of Living maximizing Programs to increase aggregate Consumption; raising Profits for private industry. The above statement is not necessarily the advocacy of Welfare transfer payments. This Country needs an additional Ten Infantry Divisions operational; this could be accomplished with half-time Service for regular Military, with a smaller Military Budget than at Present. Other like venues can be found.

This Author previously (PROGNOSIS 2000, Xlibirs, 1999) advocated a Farmland Bank, where the Federal Government would purchase all land along the River systems of the Country, back One-quarter mile from the water flow. The advantages of the Farmland Bank would be to cut extreme flooding to One-half with proper Conservation, cut the water pollution of Our River systems by Forty percent, and increase Our fresh water reserves by almost Fifty percent. The Cost would not exceed Farm payments made to Farmers for this land, over a Thirty year Period. Recreational activities would be benefitted, and the wildlife along the River systems can be estimated to at least double. The land would still be present for use, and could be leased to Farmers upon need. The construction of housing along Flood planes would also be eliminated in greatest part; while controlling the development of excess Recreational facilities. It is an idea which needs consideration.

The Conservation of Fresh Water supplies has also been discussed by the Author, and will become a vital issue in the new Century. New England is already enduring a Four year drought, with little snowfall in the current Winter. New Englanders are praying for heavy Spring rains. The South also suffers from shortages of Rainfall in many areas. A Program of Water Resource Management must be undertaken by the Federal Government. Such a Program will grow in importance; and probably absorb $30 Billion per year, as water shortages appear. The regulation of industries on the basis of water use, has to come. Fresh Water Transfer systems must be designed, by which Drinking water can be supplied for long periods of time, at the minimum. Water Purification systems need be designed with Pipeline transfer of product; which can be built within a Six month period; though construction would be a waste, until extreme drought areas are defined. El Nino is upon Us again!

A Internet Correspondent presented the Worry that the new Census identified 71 Million working age Americans, without Employment. The Author explained half were in some way medically disabled; and could not easily return to the Work force. He went on to explain the other half had left the Labor force in the late 1990s, projecting to live off the return of financial instruments. This was possible, given the high rates of return during these years. This financial return is expected to be cut by half, due to Economic slowdown. Such a slowdown is not an absolute given, and the American Economy expresses great resiliency; Profits may begin to regain the highs of 1998. The fact remains the Economy could not produce more than about 7 Million jobs per year, other than Part-times Seasonal work. This indicates the Economy could possibly handle about One-fifth of the Problem per year; then only under terms of High Consumption patterns.

The Federal Government has huge opportunities for effective Employment in huge numbers. Effective Employment can be defined as long-term benefit for both the Economy, and the Standard of Living. Clearing and dredging the River systems, along with re-surfacing the banks back One-Quarter mile; could employ a Labor force larger than the U.S. Military, with One-Quarter the Capital Equipment cost, and with a total budget of Forty percent of the current Military Budget. Conservatives would criticize this Program; but it would effectively triple the fresh water reserves. It additionally would maintain the Consumption pattern of Five Million people, and provide a possible .06 % of Corporate profits; while lowering Unemployment payments and other welfare assistance.

Construction of Condominiums for the Poor would potentially raise Construction employment by Thirty percent; while alleviating a pressing need in most major Cities. Forcing the Poor to buy their homes, at rates consuming most of their assistance payments; will enjoin them to maintain the residential value, and seek employment. The gain for the Federal Budget lies in being the Mortgage-holder; the Federal regains most of the cost of construction, with a return of most of the welfare assistance extended. Extended employment is realized, welfare assistance is minimized, pressure for gainful employment is applied; all for little more than the cost of Construction, which can be somewhat recouped. The Poor will gain in aggregate Capital holdings, though they may need to be forced; while gainful Employment is extended, with Corporate Construction profits magnified.

Leasing vehicle practices by the Federal Government should be discontinued; leasing contracts are written to profit the Product provider. The Federal Government should purchase outright, and provide resale themselves; subcontractor dealers could be obtained to sell the vehicles for the Federal Government, charging only the Salesman's fees. Purchase of fully-equipped vehicles would provide the same ease of Sale, as is currently available to lease agents. The Government could set the Prices for these vehicles, so the production of Transport can be maximized; while at the same time, providing a greater return on these vehicles for the Federal Government. The Federal Budget could derive a potential $1 Billion saving, while also enhancing Economic performance and higher Consumption rates.

The elimination of excesses in Civil Service Pay packages, as well as excess Profits-taking by Government contractors; drains much of the Inflation pressure from the Economy, the Federal Government being the largest Consumer in the American economy. This alone could reduce the real Tax impact throughout the Economy, by as much as Two percent; considering the normalized Wage spread, lessened Resource costs, and lower Federal outlays. Every .04% of reduced real Tax impact, doubles the Savings rate of Working class labor; though this is mostly translated as non-Credit accumulation of Consumer Goods and Homes. The process, though, still retains high value in furthering economic performance overall.

Conclusion

No Economist can analyze the Federal Budget; he would only find himself rummaging through a tenth of the document, by the time it was supplanted by a new Budget. Research institutions and foundations generally run Three to Seven years behind in their surveillance of Federal budgets, their own organizations staffed substantially. Most such Supervisors focus on some specific aspect of the Budget, and still run about Two years behind the current operating Budget. The Government, itself, runs on the simple process of compilation, each department submitting their own proposed budget; all of which are simply added together, without significant study. Congress takes this Compilation, subtracted Five percent from various areas, and makes up the decrease with Pork Barrel spending. All departments understand the 'Chop and Hack' process of Congressional review, so simply inflate their budgets by Ten percent. The essential movement and composition of the Budget remains ignored.

The Author attempted no numbers analysis in this Work, knowing too well the futility of such effort. Any statistics presented would be immediately challenged, by Government or Researcher trapped along the path or One or another of the last several years' budgets. Federal budget analysis has become highly noted for throwing around numeral years to justify one or another point. The Author does not lay pretension to the claim the information he did provide, even applies to the current years. He will only state what information was provided, held truth in some period of the Author's Youth. He will also state the information probably still applies Today, understanding the proclivities of Federal operations.

Government still holds the most opportune venue for both Theft and Corruption. Most Economists would not challenge a statement, at least Three percent of every Federal Budget consists of the Organized theft of Taxpayers' funds. The Author did not assert these Economists would make such a Charge themselves. This they would not do! They, like the Author, cannot prove what We know to be true. The absence of documented malfeasance generates Silence.

The wastage of Federal use of Property probably carries a $100 Billion per year additional bill for the American Economy. This can be attributed to the loss of State and Local tax revenues, as well as loss of Productive capacity. Military Reserve land alone, laying fallow; likely exceeds the farm acreage of Our smallest State. The capacity of Military stores engenders a vast waste of Warehouse capacity; while the material stored recycled, could probably sell for an amount greater than the State budgets of some of Our less populous States. Federal excess (empty) office space probably stands as Seven times the Private Sector average. Federal Property maintenance costs exceed Private Sector averages, while Deterioration rates are far higher than the Private Sector, when determined by the frequency of Remodeling and Reconstruction. The Costs go on and on.

No Government welfare benefit program has maintained it's influence on Clientele Standard of Living, since the early 1970s. This means the benefit to Recipients has been deteriorating in impact, confronted by the growth of the Economy and the resident Inflation, throughout the Period. The Operating Cost of running these welfare benefit programs has been rising faster than the Inflation rate, every Year in the same Period. These programs have been altered to promote the Civil Service Employees, not the disadvantaged.

Much Talk surrounds of the great gains of Military 'smart weapons', with the saving of human life through their use. This Author will probably be nuked for this statement; but 'smart weapons' show only a Seven percent increase in Accuracy over weapons of Vietnam War vintage, though they cost Twelve times more, and Trillions have been spend on them. Proper usage of Vietnam War vintage weaponry could give the same saving of human life; at a Tenth of the Cost, with Eight times the number of weapons being produced. The entire discussion reminds of Used Car Salesmen hawking their wares.

Study of Government Contracts fulfillment over the previous Thirty years, express one glaring fact: A decline of actual Costs going to Labor Costs, with Corporate Profits from such Contracts rising at almost Twice the rate of the Labor Costs decline. The amazing factor of the above Equation lists Capital Equipment Costs remaining almost unchanged, when scaled for the increase of Monetary payments for Contract fulfillment. It has already been stated the produced product, at least of Military weaponry, costs almost Twelve times as much. Civilian-use products from such Contracts have risen by almost Four times. Almost all of this growth in expense seems to go to Management salaries, benefits, and Stock Options; as well as Stockholder dividends. Standard Economic doctrine claim this as principles of the New Economy. The Author has some doubts.

Appendix

Normal Cash Flow And Real Tax Impact

More conventional Economists need a formal framework, to lay out Economic theory. This can become quite dull for the average Reader; so be forewarned! The easiest method generally progresses with the definition of Variables, presentation of the thesis in formula form, then explanation of the various components.

I = Income level for the entire Class

aI = average level of Income within the Class

t = tax amount for the entire Class

at = average tax on the Individuals in the Class

N = un-adjustable living expenses for the entire Class

aN = average un-adjustable living expenses for the Individual in the Class

iee = income earning expense for the entire Class

$aiee$ = average income earning expense for the Individual in the Class

$E = (N + iee)$ total un-adjustable expenses for the Class

$aE = (aN + aiee)$ average un-adjustable expenses for the Individual in the Class

$D = (I - E)$ discretionary income total for the Class.

$aD = (aI - aE)$ average discretionary income for the Individual in the Class

RD = Real discretionary income after taxes $(I - (t + E)$

aRD = Real discretionary income after taxes (al − a(t + E))

Formulas:

I30k − (t + E)30k = RD30k

al30k − (at + aE)30k = aRD30k

I40k − (t + E)40k = RD40k

al40k − (at + aE)40k = aRD40k

"   "

"   "

I100+k − (t +E)100k+ = RD100+k

al100+k − (at + aE)100+k = aRD100+k

Normal Cash Flow and Real Tax Impact theory basically states the Real Tax impact, along with the percentage of Real Tax Impact, should be equal throughout all Tax Classes. The basic formula presentation is:

RD30k/I30k = RD40k/I40k = RD50k/I50k = RD60k/I60k = RD70k/I70k = RD80k/I80k = RD90k/I90k = RD100+k/I100+k

The formula for the average percentage of Real Tax Impact is basically identical. Normal Cash Flow, according to the theory, does not warp under equalized Real Tax impact among the different Income classes; therefore, there is no more than normal borrowing—for long-term Capital aggregation—and excess Interest charges are not built up in the system The saved Interest charges throughout the Economic system contain sufficient magnitude, to produce a 3.1 percent growth in the normal Economy; absent of other Economic distortions. This growth rate should be occasioned with a lack of Inflation.

The Author must now present so many Caveats, many will come to consider him a Cow Flop specialist. The Analysis will not work for Income classes, whose discretionary income does not exceed Fifteen percent of their total Income. Many Economists would state this does not include many of the Classes listed. Homeowners with mortgages, though, must be thought equal to Investors, in the total of the Mortgage payment over and above the minimum amount necessary to rent equivalent housing. This part of the Mortgage payment must be construed as discretionary income. Business mortgages and expenses must be construed as Income Earning Expense; but only in the level of payments per year, not in the total Debt load against the Income. Tax Credits against that Debt Load eschew the equalities of Real Tax Impact, and disrupt the Normal Cash Flow. Individuals with income levels insufficient for 15+% of total Income devoted to discretionary spending, actually improve their Income potential through borrowing; the Interest paid on this borrowing remains only Income Earning Expense. Government welfare payments act in the same manner as the above borrowing; the Income Earning Expense borne by the Government.

The Kennedy Tax Cut, the Reagan Tax Cut, and the Bush Tax Cut all violated the equality ratios of Real Tax Impact; reducing the tax impact upon the wealthier classes and businesses. The Kennedy Tax Cut granted Corporations, larger Sole Proprietorships, and wealthier Individuals the ability to aggregate funds for the internal financing of operations; this effectively equated to an Eight percent reduction in Income Earning Expenses for these entities. The Reagan Tax Cut basically allowed these same entities to deduct this internal financing from their taxes. Corporations and Business actually reduced their real tax impact by half through the combination of both Tax Cuts; while cutting their Income Earning Expense to the quarter of it's per-1963 level. The Bush Tax Cut would further cut their nominal tax rate, allow for shift of Income Overseas without penalty or tax, and actually pay them for internal financing.

Many Economists claim the Vietnam War was accountable for the inflation of the 1960s, and the Oil Crisis responsible for the inflation of the 1970s. This Author believes them to be wrong. Consumer Debt increased overall throughout the period after the Kennedy tax cut, faster than the rate of Inflation. Un-adjustable living expenses increased at the same rate throughout; indicating none of the increase in Consumer Debt was actual Income Earning Expense. The Inflation of the Period simply reflected loss of discretionary spending power, increased un-adjustable living expenses, and the accumulation of debt (which was not income producing). The inflation rates equated directly in increase, to the increases of Interest payments on Debt which lacked Income-earning potential. The Interest payments of this order simply signified future draft on Goods and Services gained by non-productive function—Inflation.

The Reagan Tax Cut immediately brought a huge increase in the Interest accrued from Debt contracted in this Country. Measures were taken to slow Inflation, which started to depress the Economy. The S&L Bailout, with an equally bad posture for Banks, expressed the inability of the Economy to sustain the level of non-productive draft of resources. The Reagan Miracle was actually the Reagan Debacle; doubling the National Debt without economic gain.

The Bush Tax Cut and Economic package thinks to maximize all the basic disincentives of the previous Tax Cuts, in the interest of Profit-taking for the wealthier classes. Actual Corporate tax payments in Dollar terms have been dropping since 1998, even though Productivity has been advancing throughout the Period. The Bush Plan would double the rate of drop in actual Corporate tax collections. Investors have enjoyed about a 1.3% drop in actual Capital Gains collections since 1994. Clinton had functionally raised the total Capital Gains tax collections by almost one-third in 1993; only 77% of actual tax collections in 1962—when scaled for actual Capital Gains earned. The Bush Tax Plan would cut Capital Gains tax collections in half. All of the lost collections will push for higher Tax impact on the lower classes, or increase the National Debt.

The entire thesis behind Normal Cash Flow and Real Tax Impact maintains only equal real Tax impact between Income classes, can forestall the encumbrance of non-productive debt; whose Interest equates directly as Inflation. This is true for this debt, whether it is contracted by Consumers, or by the Government itself. This Author finishes with the statement: The only Economic stimulus exercised in the last Forty years was the Clinton Tax Increase. This Tax Increase alone brought sustainable, rapid economic growth. The Kennedy and Reagan Tax Cuts only brought Inflation—often in double digits; and the Bush Tax Cut and Economic Stimulus Package can be expected to produce worse results than the late 1980s.

0-595-22096-7

www.ingramcontent.com/pod-product-compliance
Lightning Source LLC
Chambersburg PA
CBHW030850180526
45163CB00004B/1516